# Mates, Dates and You

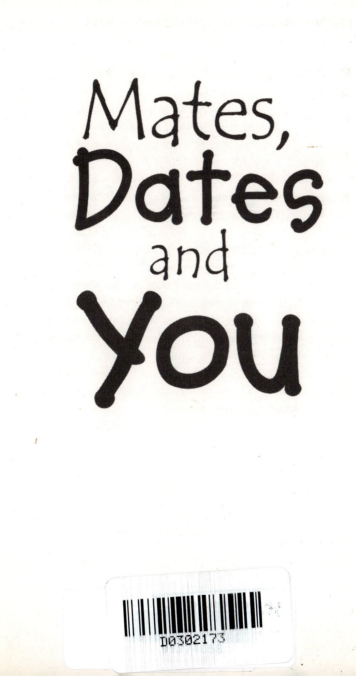

**Cathy Hopkins** is the author of the incredibly successful *Mates, Dates* and *Truth, Dare* books, and has just started a fabulous new series called *Cinnamon Girl*. She lives in North London with her husband and three cats, Molly, Emmylou and Otis.

Cathy spends most of her time locked in a shed at the bottom of the garden pretending to write books but is actually in there listening to music, hippie dancing and talking to her friends on e-mail.

Occasionally she is joined by Molly, the cat who thinks she is a copy-editor and likes to walk all over the keyboard rewriting and deleting any words she doesn't like.

Emmylou and Otis are new to the household. So far they are as insane as the older one. Their favourite game is to run from one side of the house to the other as fast as possible, then see if they can fly if they leap high enough off the furniture. This usually happens at three o'clock in the morning and they land on anyone who happens to be asleep at the time.

Apart from that, Cathy has joined the gym and spends more time than is good for her making up excuses as to why she hasn't got time to go.

# Mates, Dates and You

*Ultimate quizzes to reveal the real you!*

## Cathy Hopkins

and Vic Parker

PICCADILLY PRESS · LONDON

*Thanks as always to all at Piccadilly and to the
team of people who worked on this in particular:
Vic Parker, Sue Hellard and Anne Clark, who are now
**Mates, Dates** experts supreme!*

First published in Great Britain in 2007
by Piccadilly Press Ltd, 5 Castle Road,
London NW1 8PR

A catalogue record for this book is available from the British Library

ISBN: 978 1 85340 908 0 (trade paperback)

1 3 5 7 9 10 8 6 4 2

Printed and bound by Bookmarque Ltd
Designed by Fiona Webb
Cover design by Simon Davis

# Contents

## SECTION 3: So you think you know Mates, Dates?

## SECTION 4: Mad match-ups and mini-quizzes

# Introduction

This book is packed with fabulous quizzes to reveal the real you.

Section 1 helps you discover which of the four *Mates, Dates* girls you are most like. Are you a dead ringer for Lucy? Are you just like Izzie when it comes to falling in love? Do you and TJ share lots of interests? Or are you as confident as Nesta? Find out your secret soul sister by answering the questions.

In Section 2, the girls (and Tony) put your personality through its paces. Find out what kind of friend you are and what kind of boy would suit you best. Learn more about your spiritual and social sides, and find out if you're a goddess girlriend or a dating disaster!

If you think you know all about *Mates, Dates*, Section 3 puts your memory to the test with questions about all the people, places and happenings from the books. With three levels to attempt, from easy-peasy to fiendishly difficult, find out if you're a true *Mates, Dates* expert.

Section 4 rounds things off with a lucky dip of match-ups, anagrams and mini-quizzes.

So dive in and enjoy!

# SECTION 1

# Who are you most like?

Have you ever thought about which girl you're most like: Lucy, Izzie, Nesta or TJ? These quizzes will reveal how you compare with the *Mates, Dates* friends - in looks, in personality and in love.

# Who are you most like ... in looks?

**1. How would you best describe your complexion?**

| | | |
|---|---|---|
| ★ | English rose | 1 |
| ★ | Olive or coffee | 3 |
| ★ | An outdoor, healthy glow | 4 |
| ★ | Pale and interesting | 2 |

**2. What is your hair like?**

| | | |
|---|---|---|
| ★ | Long, straight and salon-stunning | 3 |
| ★ | Long and wild, but wonderful | 4 |
| ★ | Shoulder-length, mussed up and mysterious | 2 |
| ★ | Short and sassy | 1 |

**3. What do you like to do with your hair?**

| | | |
|---|---|---|
| ★ | Try funky new cuts and colours | 1 |
| ★ | Tie it out of the way | 4 |
| ★ | Leave it glossy and swinging | 3 |
| ★ | Accessorise with clips, clasps and hats | 2 |

## 4. What colour are your eyes?

★ Amber         4
★ Blue         1
★ Chestnut         3
★ Green         2

## 5. How would you best describe your figure?

★ I'd say fat, friends say curvy    2
★ Petite    1
★ Athletic    4
★ Voluptuous    3

## 6. What do you like best about your body?

★ My luscious lips    4
★ My cheekbones and fine facial features    1
★ My unusual eyes (third eye included!)    2
★ My model height    3

## 7. Which body part do you dislike the most?

★ My 30-A chest    1
★ My expanding thighs and bum    2
★ My big feet    3
★ My generous cleavage    4

*ergh!*

## 8. What is your favourite style of clothes?

★ Anything different, whether goth or goddess   2
★ Anything comfy   4
★ Anything designer   3
★ Anything I've customised myself   1

## 9. What is your favourite type of shoe?

★ Nikes or Converse All Stars   4
★ Anything which says Jimmy Choo, Prada or Christian Louboutin on the insole   3
★ Anything with a three-inch heel   1
★ Anything non-leather, preferably with massage bubbles on the insole to stimulate my reflexology points   2

## 10. What type of bag are you most likely to carry?

★ A boho bag from the market   2
★ One of my mum's designer clutches   3
★ A unique one-off creation of my own   1
★ A sports bag   4

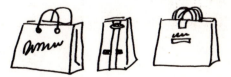

## 11. What accessory would you never be seen dead without?

★ A wonderbra    1
★ Some sunglasses    3
★ A hairclip     4
★ A healing crystal (like rose quartz)    2

## 12. Which celebrity do you most closely resemble?

★ Angelina Jolie    4
★ Beyoncé Knowles    3
★ Kylie Minogue    1
★ Alanis Morissette    2

# Scores

★ *If you scored 12 to 20:*

You are most like the lovely Lucy – petite, but perfectly formed. You apply your fantastic fashion sense with an individual flair that everyone envies.

★ *If you scored 21 to 29:*

You are most like Izzie – a bootylicious beauty. You show off your curves in bold clothes that emphasise your dramatic features and strong personality.

★ *If you scored 30 to 38:*

You are most like Nesta – a natural stunner. With your model figure and drop-dead style you could make a bin liner look like a designer frock.

★ *If you scored 39 to 48:*

You are most like TJ – a voluptuous siren. Your relaxed, effortless style by day gives way to a show-stopping look by night.

# Who are you most like ... in personality?

**1. Which of these descriptions best suits you?**

★ A good mate                                    4
★ Dramatic, colourful and fun                    3
★ Sweet, gentle and funny                        1
★ Weird, rebellious and wise                     2

**2. What do you think about when you daydream?**

★ What my life will be like when I'm rich and
  famous                                         3
★ God and the meaning of the universe            2
★ The characters and plot of my latest story     4
★ Snogging and the plight of endangered
  orang-utans in Borneo – but not snogging
  orang-utans, obviously!                        1

### 3. What is your best quality?

★ I have a great sense of humour and am good at easing tension between people   1

★ I am diplomatic and a good communicator   4

★ I instinctively know what's bothering people   2

★ I have lots of get-up-and-go   3

### 4. What is your worst quality?

★ I have a tendency to put my foot in it   3

★ I lack self-confidence   4

★ I am so passionate I can become obsessed by my interests and beliefs   2

★ I can expect too much from my friends   1

### 5. Which word describes you best?

★ Ambitious   3

★ Intuitive   2

★ Creative   1

★ Brainbox   4

### 6. Which of these problems do you suffer most from?

★ Not thinking before I speak   3

★ Blushing   1

★ Being addicted to chocolate   2

★ Being too shy to talk to boys   4

**7.   Which of these would upset you most?**

★ Bad news on TV, like wars, famine and stuff  2

★ Failing an exam  4

★ Having no mates  1

★ Losing my boy magnetism  3

**8.   Which of these animals do you like best?**

★ Horse  1

★ Cat  3

★ Penguin  4

★ Dolphin  2

**9.   Which of these sayings would you choose as your motto?**

★ The road of life is always under construction  4

★ You'll never learn to sing if you're not prepared to open your mouth and hit a few bum notes  2

★ Look for the rainbow in every storm  1

★ Life is not a rehearsal  3

**10.  What are your friends most likely to nickname you?**

★ Big-mouth  3

★ Wise woman  2

★ Babe-with-brains                                      4
★ Mini-me                                               1

## 11. What would you most like to change about yourself?

★ I'd like to do more to help sad and lonely people around me (and grow a chest! Boobs that is, not a hairy one)                1
★ I'd like to be more confident around boys             4
★ I'd like not to lose my cool or independence over a boy                                          2
★ I'd like to be a 'deeper' person                      3

## 12. If you were to star in a movie, which movie would best suit you?

★ *Bewitched*                                           2
★ *Catwoman*                                            3
★ *The Wizard of Oz* (playing lead Munchkin)            1
★ *Lara Croft, Tomb Raider*                             4

# Scores

★ *If you scored 12 to 20:*
You are most like the bright, bubbly Lucy. One of
your main strengths is your fantastic sense of
humour, which never fails to either dissolve tension
or cheer people up. Your mates are extremely
important to you – you're an outstandingly loyal,
reliable friend – and you're always looking further
afield to help others in need, whether it's lonely
people or neglected animals.

★ *If you scored 21 to 29:*
You are most like mystical, mysterious Izzie. In
touch with your spiritual side, you have a sixth sense
where people close to you are involved and you are
very concerned with the well-being of the world in
general. Your attempts to focus on the higher things
in life sometimes fall by the wayside when you're
tempted by more earthly passions – chocolate, boys,
and more chocolate. But hey, everyone has their
weaknesses . . .

★ *If you scored 30 to 38:*

You are most like dynamic diva Nesta. Always full of get up and go, you know what you want and you're not afraid to reach out to get it. Others envy your seemingly boundless confidence, but they don't realise you've had your troubles just like everyone else, and have had to work hard to build your self-esteem. They also don't remember the times when you get carried away and end up putting your foot in it! But that's what star quality is all about – dazzling others with your best bits!

★ *If you scored 39 to 48:*

You are most like the talented TJ. Inwardly unconfident and shy, outwardly you seem to other people to have it all – the looks, the intelligence, the personality, the friends and the self-assurance. For a career, you'd like to make an impact, but not in a showy, in-the-limelight way. You'd make an excellent writer, teacher, doctor or lawyer (for the last two, especially where underprivileged or vulnerable people are concerned).

13

# Who are you most like ... in personal tastes?

**1.  What is your favourite food?**

★  Potato wedges and sour cream                3
★  Chunky chips                                4
★  Ben & Jerry's Chunky Monkey ice cream       1
★  Broccoli (yeah, right – more like chocolate) 2

**2.  Which of these drinks do you prefer?**

★  Hot chocolate with marshmallows             1
★  Coke                                        3
★  Elderflower juice                           2
★  Banana milkshake with vanilla
   ice cream, yum                              4

**3.  Which of these activities are you most
      likely to do in your spare time?**

★  *Feng Shui* in my bedroom                   2
★  Go shopping or on a café cruise             3
★  Play tennis or other sports                 4
★  Read mags or watch a romantic movie         1

## 4. Which of these colours do you like best?

★ Black                                           3
★ Any shade of blue                               1
★ Silver                                          2
★ Violet                                          4

## 5. Which of these movies would you prefer to watch?

★ *Breakfast at Tiffany's*                        3
★ *It's a Wonderful Life*                         4
★ *The Sixth Sense*                               2
★ *Sleepless in Seattle*                          1

## 6. Which of the following would you prefer to read?

★ *Hello!* magazine                               3
★ The *Narnia* books by CS Lewis                  1
★ *Junk* by Melvin Burgess                        2
★ *Sense and Sensibility* by Jane Austen          4

## 7. What sort of wedding is your dream 'big day'?

★ A celeb-packed ceremony in a big, posh mansion  3
★ A candlelit church wedding just before Christmas 1

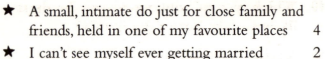
★ A small, intimate do just for close family and
   friends, held in one of my favourite places    4

★ I can't see myself ever getting married    2

**8. What couldn't you live without?**

★ My mates    2
★ My lip-gloss    3
★ Air (ha ha ha)    1
★ My dog/cat/other pet pal    4

**9. What would be the best way to cheer
yourself up if you were having a crapola
time?**

★ Spend the day with my mates, having
   a laugh    1

★ Crack open my piggy bank and hit the shops  3

★ Bash the hell out of a squash ball and
   then settle down with a really good book    4

★ Chocolate and aromatherapy    2

**10. Which type of book would you be most likely to take out of the library?**

★ A book on horoscopes     2

★ A book on fashion through the ages     1

★ A book on interesting people or places     4

★ Where's the library?     3

**11. Which of these is your secret talent?**

★ Reading Tarot cards     2

★ Arm-wrestling     4

★ Spotting ratfink boys     3

★ Doing fashion makeovers     1

**12. Which of these would you prefer to do when you're grown up?**

★ To be a famous actress (or possibly model, I haven't quite decided yet)     3

★ To be a fashion designer or celebrity stylist     1

★ To be a successful writer     4

★ To be a singer and travel the world     2

# Scores

★ *If you scored 12 to 20:*

You are most like Lucy – your best times are spent with your mates, having a laugh, but you also enjoy being on your own doing creative, self-expressive hobbies. You have a taste for romance, and you find comfort in your favourite childhood things, such as ice cream and magical stories.

★ *If you scored 21 to 29:*

You are most like Izzie. You care equally about your mind, body and spirit, and as such, you like to nourish yourself with all things healthy and wholesome (with the odd bit of chocolate thrown in now and again). You're drawn towards mystical, magical pursuits, following hobbies that explore the unknown side of life. However, you also have a very down-to-earth, practical streak which means you like getting involved in combating life's grim realities too, e.g. campaigning against war or to stop racism.

★ *If you scored 30 to 38:*

You are most like Nesta. You have expensive, designer tastes and are drawn to the high life. You have a fascination with celebrity – though you wish you didn't, because you are worried this is shallow. You are passionate about performance arts, such as acting/modelling/singing/dancing – but this is as much because you wish to be famous and wealthy as it is because you enjoy these pursuits and have natural talent for them. You prefer to be up and doing, interacting with people, rather than being on your own, contemplating.

★ *If you scored 39 to 48:*

You are most like TJ. You crave activities that allow you to stretch yourself physically and intellectually, so you enjoy both active hobbies such as sports and more 'brainy' interests such as books, movies and writing. You can easily feel intimidated, so you prefer to be in familiar surroundings with people you know well and trust. You like classic books, movies and styles, and also exploring brand new works that stimulate your own ideas.

# Who are you most like … in family?

**1.  How long have your parents been together?**

★ Since the dawn of time – my parents are
   older than most                                    4

★ Since before I was born (ha ha) –
   my parents met when they were students      1

★ They aren't together                                2

★ An average length of time I s'pose                  3

**2.  How much like your parents do you think you are?**

★ I am like one of them, the other was a
   visiting alien                                      2

★ Bit like both (bleurgh, I don't like to think
   that they ever had sex, eeew, eeew, eeew)          1

★ Nothing like either of them, we are totally
   different generations!                              4

★ I've inherited the best of both of them!            3

### 3. How close are your siblings (including half- and step-siblings) to you in age?

★ Much older sibling/s     4

★ Much younger sibling/s     2

★ One sibling, fairly close to me in age     3

★ Two or more siblings, fairly close to me in age     1

★ I am an only child     4

### 4. If you have them, how do you feel about your siblings?

★ OK, as long as I don't have to use the bathroom after them     1

★ I care a lot about my siblings     2

★ I get on well with them although we are different     4

★ I'd like to thump them most of the time     3

### 5. When your parents aren't at work, what are they most likely to be doing with their time?

★ Eating lentil pie and listening to jazz     1

★ Cleaning and house maintenance     2

★ Reading the *Telegraph*, listening to Radio 4 or relaxing in the garden     4

★ Eating out, going to the theatre, or watching a movie together     3

**6. What are you most likely to argue about with your parents?**

★ My friends coming round and making too much noise and mess                                4

★ My annoying siblings                                3

★ Being fed mung beans and tofu when I'd rather have burger and chips                                1

★ Being fed burger and chips when I'd rather have mung beans and tofu                                2

**7. When your friends visit, what are your parents most likely to say as they come through the door?**

★ Shoes off, please!                                2

★ Fancy a cappuccino?                                3

★ Why don't you go straight up to your bedroom, dear? (subtext: out of our way)                                4

★ Hello, love, clear a space and make yourself at home                                1

**8. How would your friends be most likely to describe your family?**

★ Old-fashioned                                4

★ Cool                                3

★ Laid back                                1

★ Are we talking about Family One or Family Two?                                2

## 9. How modern are your parents?

★ They think they're modern, but they're stuck in the Seventies     1

★ They're totally out of date and they don't mind     4

★ They're up to date with modern technology, music, design, etc.     3

★ Both are well teched up, but one's more classic and the other more boho than modern     2

## 10. Which of these hobbies would your parents be most likely to try?

★ Growing organic fruit and veg     1
★ Photography     3
★ Reading     2
★ Touring stately homes and gardens     4

## 11. If you could change one thing about your parents, what would it be?

★ I would make them less serious     4
★ I would like them to get on together better     2
★ I would change their embarrassing sense of style     1
★ I would make them way richer     3

style arsenal

## 12. **Which of these best describes your relationship with your family?**

★ Pretty good, we talk about most stuff    3

★ They care for me and trust me but are slightly distant; they live in their world, and I live in mine    4

★ We all get on when we have time together amidst the madness    1

★ Never a dull moment – lots of disagreements but we do love each other underneath    2

# Scores

★ *If you scored 12 to 20:*
You are most like Lucy. You have a loving, liberal family, made up of very strong and different individual personalities. Your family drives you wild at times, but they allow you to be yourself and support you in whatever you do. Your friends envy you because they think your family is cool.

★ *If you scored 21 to 29:*
You are most like Izzie. You don't fit into the conventional picture of a mum, a dad and 2.4 kids – you're either living with just one parent, or guardians, or you have two or more families and often find yourself with divided loyalties. You often feel very different from your family, but you know that life would be very dull if everyone was the same. So you embrace everyone's uniqueness and life's imperfections – as long as they embrace yours!

★ *If you scored 30 to 38:*
You are most like Nesta. You feel comfortable with your parents because you admire, and to a certain extent share, their tastes and interests. You also have a lot in common with your sibling/s – although this

can get under your skin at times. Your friends are relaxed around your parents, because they have their finger on the pulse of modern life, without trying too hard to be young, trendy and cool.

### ★ *If you scored 39 to 48:*
You are most like TJ. You have a safe and secure family but sometimes feel rather isolated all the same. You love and respect your parents, even though they don't really understand you and your mates (but they do try their best). However, your mates think your parents would be great to turn to in a crisis – as dependable and solid as rock.

# Who are you most like … in fashion and beauty?

**1. Do you have a particular fashion style?**

★ Yep – it's all my own creation     1

★ Whatever's hot 'n' happenin'     3

★ Different from the crowd though I like cyber-babe or rock chick     2

★ More Buffy than Barbie, but I don't really think much about fashion     4

**2. How do you feel about make-up?**

★ I don't mind a bit of lip-gloss now and again, but overall, I prefer the natural look     4

★ I'm fond of goth eyes and scarlet lippy     2

★ I'm happy going without during the day, but for the evening I love to try out the latest shimmering colours     1

★ I'm stunning without make-up, but even more stunning with     3

## 3. What would you do if you fancy giving yourself a face-mask?

★ Make your own DIY gloop and invite all
  your mates round for a pampering sesh      1
★ Nick one of my mum's posh ones            3
★ Buy an aromatherapy one                   2
★ Buy a silver one and go to Venice for the
  masked ball                               4

## 4. What's the best thing about going to the gym?

★ Relaxing in the sauna afterwards, particularly
  if someone's put eucalyptus oil in the burner  2
★ The fit-looking gym instructors            3
★ Being the fastest on the running machines  4
★ Showing off my customised gym kit          1

## 5. What is your ideal style of wedding dress?

★ Something classy and elegant               4
★ Something outrageous, like a red rubber dress
  and rollerblades                           2
★ Something silky, slinky and sexy           3
★ Something romantic with vintage lace
  and tiny seed pearls                       1

**6.** **Which of these is most like the worst fashion disaster you have ever had?**

★ I had a disastrous haircut     1

★ I got too big for all my clothes     2

★ I was given a makeover by my mates and they made me look like a drag queen     4

★ I had to have a brace fitted     3

**7.** **What is the worst thing that could happen to you, fashion-wise, in the world?**

★ Combat trousers go out of style     4

★ I have to wear nun's kit     3

★ Black goes out of style     2

★ The Government passes a law saying that everyone has to wear the same thing     1

**8.** **What is the best thing that could happen to you, fashion-wise, in the world?**

★ Curvy figures become the height of fashion – especially big bottoms     2

★ I am spotted by a scout from a top model agency and offered a contract on the spot to be the next big catwalk sensation     3

★ My custom-made clothes are spotted by a scout from a fashion label and I am offered a contract on the spot to be a designer     1

★ Sportswear becomes the height of fashion     4

9. **You're giving yourself some 'me' time and are trying to relax and meditate. What soothing, calming, contented pictures do you conjure up?**

★ The perfume counters in Selfridges, rails of fab clothes in Morgan, the lingerie department in Selfridges and a snogathon with a boy babe (actually, cut the first three)     3

★ A picnic on a sunny day with mates and marshmallows     1

★ Wandering around a stately home on a private tour     4

★ Swimming with dolphins and a healing turquoise light radiating through your body     2

10. **What would be your motivation to clear out all your old clothes from your bedroom?**

★ To take it to the charity shop, so everyone will see what a fab caring sharing person I am! (And modest too!)     3

★ It's good *Feng Shui* to clear the clutter     2

★ To see what boring old stuff I've got that – with a bit of imagination – I can recycle into fantastic new outfits     1

★ To keep my parents from nagging me     4

## 11. How would you deal with unwanted body hair?

★ Waxing (arghhh)     1

★ Bleaching     4

★ Laser hair removal     3

★ Sugaring (or go hairy like ze French, oo la la) 2

## 12. What would you wear to a glam event like a ball?

★ A gorgeous vintage dress I found on a stall in Portobello Road market     1

★ A long black velvet dress, with diamanté choker and deep red lipstick     2

★ A purple basque with black trousers and glam earrings     4

★ Something designer, with tiny straps and high heels     3

# Scores

★ *If you scored 12 to 20:*

You are most like Lucy – a style-setter, rather than a trend-follower. You look everywhere and anywhere for inspiration, take ideas, and then make them your own. You don't feel you have to be dressed up all the time, but one of your main pleasures in your spare time is experimenting with new outfits and different looks for hair and make-up. You know that pampering beauty treatments can soothe your soul as well as improve your body, and you enjoy indulging yourself and your mates with healthy home-made concoctions.

★ *If you scored 21 to 29:*

You are most like Izzie. You like making bold, dramatic statements with your individual look, which can range from classic all-black clothes and scarlet lipstick, to weird and wonderful cyber-babe. You are a firm believer in the adage that beauty comes from the inside, so you know it's important to nourish your spiritual well-being as well as your physical well-being. If you are inwardly happy and at peace, you will shine outwardly – no matter what you're wearing and no matter what your physical imperfections.

### ★ *If you scored 30 to 38:*

You are most like Nesta. You are confident about your looks and know that, when you want to impress, you have the assets and the fashion know-how to really turn it on. You don't think that sweating it out at the gym is essential, but you do feel that expensive, hi-tech beauty products have real benefits, and a day at a good spa can work wonders. You appreciate couture and designer wear, and know that you are one of the lucky few who can carry off these clothes – and how! But, you know you look drop-dead gorgeous in high-street too . . .

### ★ *If you scored 39 to 48:*

You are most like TJ. You have a range of favourite clothes you feel comfortable in and you know suits you, and you're quite happy to stick with this style even though fashions come and go. You would hate to go out somewhere and feel overdressed – but, if a big occasion calls for it, you'll wear a really special outfit and totally wow everybody. You are conscious of what you put into and onto your body, and you'd prefer to go *au naturel* than to slap chemical-filled lotions and potions all over your skin and hair. You love exercise because, as long as you feel fit and healthy, you feel beautiful.

# Who are you most like ... at home?

**1. What type of home do you live in?**

★ A flat     3
★ Detached house with a garden     1
★ I split my time between two or more homes   2
★ Semi-detached or terraced house with garden 4

**2. Which of these is the best thing about your home?**

★ The interesting artefacts and characterful interior     3
★ It is unpretentious and comfortable     1
★ Its lovely gardens with roses     4
★ Er ... it's clean?     2

**3. Which of these is the worst thing about your home?**

★ Its old-fashioned décor     4
★ It's always in total chaos     1

★ It's like living in a clinic 2

★ It cost mega bucks to buy 3

## 4. What is your kitchen like?

★ The largest, messiest room in the house 1

★ An elegant, comfortable kitchen-diner
with breakfast bar 3

★ Seriously out of date 4

★ All gleaming stainless steel, polished work
surfaces, and the very latest appliances 2

## 5. What is your bathroom like?

★ Avocado suite (bleurgh!), slimy soap
(double bleurgh!) and mismatched towels 1

★ Clean, but boring, medicated soap, smells
of antiseptic 4

★ Like a five-star hotel: marble, double sink,
pristine white towels, Chanel, his and hers 2

★ Eastern style, big antique gold mirror, rich
colours, smells exotic with a mix of bath
products from all round the globe 3

**6. Which of these posters would you prefer to have on your bedroom wall?**

★ Ewan McGregor and Suzanne Vega     2
★ Orlando Bloom and a baby seal (not both on the same poster . . . duh!)     1
★ Brad, Robbie, Lemar, Justin . . . shall I continue?     3
★ Albert Einstein and Freddie Ljungberg     4

**7. How would your friends describe the atmosphere in your home?**

★ Cosmopolitan!     3
★ Unlived in     2
★ Laid-back     1
★ Like a doctor's waiting room: quiet but boring     4

**8. If you could live anywhere, where would you rather have your home?**

★ Somewhere with good spiritual vibes, like Glastonbury     2
★ Manhattan or Hollywood or both     3
★ Anywhere as long as it's near my family and friends     1
★ Somewhere scenic, such as an historical town or a seaside village     4

**9. If you could decorate your bedroom in any of the following styles, what would you choose?**

★ Moroccan style – all reds, oranges and ochres   4

★ Indian style – pale lilac, powder blue and shimmering silver, with floaty chiffon curtains and drapes   1

★ *Feng Shui* style – with healing colours such as turquoise and purple   2

★ A romantic style – but not too girlie – with muslin drapes around the bed, heaps of cushions, and beautifully scented with exotic room spray   3

**10. If you could have any sort of bathroom, what would you choose?**

★ Glam! Marble, lights, mirrors, huge shower, stacks of fluffy white towels and gleaming chrome taps, loads of lotions and potions   3

★ A Victorian-style bathroom with black-and-white floor tiles, a bath with feet in the middle of the room, and a loo with a chain   4

★ A bathroom in soothing colours, with plenty of nooks and crannies for aromatherapy candles, and full of essential oils and natural, health-giving lotions and potions   2

★ My own! Not used by dogs or siblings   1

## 11. If you could have any sort of garden, what would you choose?

★ A garden big enough for sport including a tennis court, swimming pool, croquet lawn and hammock in a shady area for reading    4

★ An organic garden with lots of fruit trees and plenty of room for a big vegetable patch and fragrant herb garden    2

★ One big enough for summer parties with a swimming pool, terraces with fabulous views and spot-lit patios    3

★ A country cottage garden that gives different bright blooms all year round, with a large barbecue and patio for parties with strings of coloured lanterns through the trees    1

## 12. If you had one word to describe your ideal home, what would it be?

★ Harmonious    2
★ Glamorous    3
★ Interesting    4
★ Stylish    1

# Scores

★ *If you scored 12 to 20:*

You are most like Lucy. You would like your home to be stylish and colourful, reflecting your individual flair and taste – but there would have to be a balance between exciting interior design and comfort. You feel that if your home isn't a welcoming, laid-back place for your family and friends to hang out, then it's not a proper home. If you could have anything at all in a house, it would be a massive walk-in wardrobe and a luxurious private bathroom – bliss!

★ *If you scored 21 to 29:*

You are most like Izzie. Your home is decorated and kitted out with impeccable taste – but it just doesn't *feel* right to you. You'd rather be surrounded by personal knick-knacks and souvenirs that you've collected over the years and which mean a lot to you (even if they look bizarre) than with fashionable objects from the latest interior design magazines. For you, a beautiful home is a healthy home. It's essential to keep the energies in your home balanced and in tune with the surrounding environment if you're going to be happy.

★ *If you scored 30 to 38:*

You are most like Nesta. Your ideal home would be elegance and luxury all the way. Its location is very important too – you need to be somewhere where there's a lot going on in the way of people, shops, cafés, clubs, theatres (although you'd happily own a small, cosy country cottage too, for weekends hiding away with your closest mates or boyfriend). You would enjoy entertaining at home, inviting interesting, vibrant people to lively dinner parties. (Cook the food yourself? Who are you kidding! You'd definitely get the caterers in . . . )

★ *If you scored 39 to 48:*

You are most like TJ. If you could have any house in the world, it would be one brimming with character – period style, rustic charm or ethnic splendour. If you could give yourself a 'dream room', it would probably be a cosy, private study, with a comfy reading chair and brimming with treasured books, and with a writing desk under a picturesque window where you could sit for hours scribbling away. Your external environment is very important to you. Your ideal home would have plenty of outdoor space – either a big, rambling garden of its own, or a large stretch of countryside or coast nearby to roam about and admire the stunning views.

# Who are you most like ... at school?

**1.  Which of the following descriptions is closest to how you feel about school?**

★ I like school and am good at most subjects    4

★ I like school and am good at some subjects    1

★ School doesn't tackle what I'm really interested in    2

★ I am one of the popular, cool ones at school    3

**2.  Which of these subjects are you best at?**

★ Art    1

★ English    4

★ Drama    3

★ Music    2

**3.  Which of these subjects do you find most frustrating?**

★ RE – it raises more questions than it answers    2

★ Cookery – something always goes wrong and my efforts end up a disaster    3

★ Maths – bo-oring     1
★ Music – I have the voice of a frog     4

**4.** **Which of these excuses would you be most likely to use if you were late to school?**

★ I'm late because someone stole the wheels off my bike     4
★ I'm late because, in my morning meditation, I went into a parallel universe where it was an hour earlier     2
★ I'm late because so many people stopped me on the way in to ask for autographs     3
★ I'm late because my annoying siblings changed the time on my alarm clock for a joke     1

**5.** **Which of the following is most like your attitude towards homework?**

★ People always ask to copy mine     4
★ I don't like homework but I try my best     1
★ It's best done with a mate – two heads are better than one     2
★ Sooner started, sooner over, then I can get on with something much more interesting     3

**6. Which of these excuses would you be most likely to use if you turned up at school without your homework?**

★ I did do my homework but when my mother cleaned up last night she must have thrown it away by mistake    2

★ I couldn't do my homework last night because I was at an audition for the new West End production of *Bugsy Malone*    3

★ I couldn't do my homework because I was representing the school at the county athletics meet    4

★ I did do my homework, but my dog/dogs/ siblings chewed it up – honest!    1

**7. How would you deal with a bully?**

★ Send them slinking away with their tail between their legs with one of your caustic, witty one-liners    3

★ Confide in your mates – there's safety in numbers    1

★ Challenge them to an arm-wrestling competition and humiliate them in front of everyone    4

★ Put a spell on them to bring them out in boils until they stop harassing you    2

43

**8. Which after-school activity would you be most likely to join in with?**

★ A sports club     4

★ T'ai chi or yoga     2

★ Rehearsals for the annual school show     3

★ A group that fundraises for a charity     1

**9. How do you cope with revision?**

★ Use Bach Flower Remedies for concentration, fish oils for braininess and essential oils of basil and peppermint to aid memory and focus     2

★ Stick key quotes, dates and formulas around the house where I can't help but see them several times a day     1

★ Set myself a certain amount a day and remind myself that as soon as it's done, I can watch a movie or read a magazine or go out for a coffee     3

★ Make a revision schedule and checklist and mark off my progress with a carefully-planned system of different-coloured highlighter pens     4

**10. What are you most likely to do on the morning of a big exam?**

★ Drink loads of coffee then regret it because I end up busting for the loo halfway through the exam     3

★ Meditate to focus my mind and remove stress 2
★ Go for a jog to shake off nerves then check I've got everything I need in the way of pencils, pens, calculators, etc. 4
★ Wear my lucky charm bracelet and pray. 1

## 11. What would you give your favourite teacher as a thank you present at the end of the year?

★ Home-made bath oil or chocs 2
★ A card with my autograph as it will be worth money some day soon 3
★ A gorgeous scarf or some earrings from the Portobello Road market 1
★ An interesting little book, such as a book of wise sayings or funny quotations 4

## 12. Which of these phrases would be most likely to appear on your school report?

★ Shows energy and enthusiasm – likes to take the lead; will go far 3
★ A caring member of the class 1
★ We love you – please stay here forever (signed The Headmaster) 4
★ Gives unique, well thought-out answers – but they tend to do the teachers' heads in 2

# Scores

★ *If you scored 12 to 20:*

You are most like Lucy. You are happy at school, doing well in some subjects and not so well in others, just like most people. You try hard with classwork and homework, because you don't want to let yourself down by not achieving your full potential, and you'd also hate to disappoint your parents. But you don't let it get you down when you have to do things you're simply not suited for – you can laugh at yourself and put disasters behind you. You are one of the most likeable, popular girls in the Year.

★ *If you scored 21 to 29:*

You are most like Izzie. You try hard at school, but, at the end of the day, the academic life isn't really for you. You can't quite understand this, because your brain is on the go all the time, and you have plenty of questions to ask the teachers – their answers just don't seem to make sense to you. For this reason, your homework is always applauded for originality and inventiveness, but you never get top marks because it's not what's expected! Your class-mates like you because you have a natural talent for exasperating the teachers and sending lessons off in unusual, entertaining directions . . .

### ★ *If you scored 30 to 38:*

You are most like Nesta. You want to do well at school, but you know that grades and exam results are just a part of your rich, full life. You don't shirk homework and exam revision, but it irritates you because you're always buzzing to do other things. Everyone knows who you are at school, because you're always involved in school drama and dance productions (usually as the lead), charity shows and PR events like fêtes and fundraisers. You are one of the cool ones at school – everyone would love to be in your circle of close mates.

### ★ *If you scored 39 to 48:*

You are most like TJ. You are confident at school, because it is an environment in which you do well. You are good at most subjects (including sports), although this sometimes makes you feel uncomfortable because you don't like standing out in the class. Everyone thinks that doing well is effortless for you – they don't realise that you put in just as much, or more, hard work and dedication than other people to get your excellent results. You are liked and admired by most other pupils, though some spiteful people envy you and would like to see you come a cropper!

# Who are you most like ... in love?

**1. How many boyfriends have you had?**

★ One to two     1
★ Three to four     4
★ Four to eight     2
★ Eight or more     3

**2. What do you think about meeting 'The One'?**

★ Who says you get only one One? If I'm lucky, I will meet The One, The Two, The Three ... 3
★ The One will be my soulmate for life     1
★ If it's meant to be, destiny will bring us together in this life as it has in past lives     2
★ It's all chemical; 'the One' is just a way of saying you fancy someone and your pheromones are mutually attractive     4

### 3. Who are you most likely to end up with as a boyfriend?

★ A boy from a group or club I go to who has mutual interests 4

★ One of my mates' brothers 1

★ A boy I can really talk to 2

★ The best-looking boy from the college down the road 3

### 4. How would you be most likely to get yourself noticed by the object of your desire?

★ By being blindingly beautiful 3

★ By hanging out outside his school, then bump into him accidentally on purpose 1

★ By showing an interest in him and laugh at his jokes, no matter how bad they are 2

★ By offering him money? God, I don't know! 4

### 5. What is your favourite flirting technique?

★ To give him a big smile to show I like what I see 2

★ To offer to arm-wrestle with him? No? 4

★ To wear something gorgeous to make him sit up and take notice 1

★ To make eye contact, look away, look back again and hold his gaze for a few seconds 3

6. **A boy you really fancy finally gets round to asking you out for Saturday night – only prob is, you've already arranged to go to the movies with your mates. What do you do?**

★ Put him off – mates come first                                1

★ Ask the Tarot cards what I should do                        2

★ Call my mates and ask what they'd do and
  hope they all say go for it, we can meet
  another time; otherwise, see if the boy wants
  to come too                                                  4

★ Tell the boy that I have a window in my
  diary for Saturday afternoon when I can
  fit him into my busy schedule – but my
  evenings are booked up for the next two
  weeks at least                                               3

7. **What would you do if you found yourself fancying your best mate's boyfriend?**

★ Agonise about it, then confide in a close
  friend and try to stop myself acting on it     4

★ Ignore how I felt. Mates' boyfriends are a
  'no go' in my book                             1

★ Try Buddhist meditation to free
  myself from the circle of desire.         2

★ Congratulate my best friend
  on her boyfriend being so lush                 3

## 8. How do you act if you are waiting for a boy to ring you?

★ Go slightly mad, write songs, eat chocolate, do a spell to MAKE him call     2

★ I never have to wait – they always ring straight away     3

★ I tell myself that the boy probably won't call – I don't want to get my hopes up and then be disappointed     4

★ I'm pretty cool – if they want to ring, they'll ring; if they don't, it's their loss     1

## 9. Have you ever been a lyin' cheatin' love rat?

★ Never, never, never     1

★ Plenty of chances have come my way – but no     3

★ Yes, unintentionally     4

★ No, because I believe in karma: what goes around comes around     2

## 10. You've just been dumped. How do you react?

★ Allow twenty-four hours of feeling sorry for myself, watch weepy movies with mates, eat ice cream, etc. then move on – there are plenty more fish in the sea   1

★ Cry, but then write it up in my journal; all these experiences can be used in my novel   4

★ Eat chocolate – loads of it, wear a healing crystal and then write a song about it   2

★ Dumped! *Moi*? OK, I'd think that it was his loss and go out and pull someone else to distract myself   3

## 11. Which of the following would be the most likely reason why you would finish with a boy?

★ I'm not ready for a serious physical relationship, or he gets too possessive – I hate that   1

★ He's great eye-candy, but his conversation is about as interesting as a goldfish's, or he's self-obsessed   4

★ Destiny brings someone even more gorgeous into my world and I can't fight fate   2

★ Kissing him is like eating cottage cheese – really boring   3

**12. Which of the following would you be most likely to do to get revenge on a no-good boy?**

★ Sew fresh prawns into his duvet     3

★ Sew up the ankles of his trousers     4

★ Tie his shoelaces together     1

★ Forgiveness is better for the soul than revenge . . . but if I was really forced to take revenge, I'd get his mobile phone and ring the talking clock in Hong Kong     2

# Scores

★ *If you scored 12 to 20:*

You are most like Lucy. You're not interested in working your way through the massive selection box of boykind that's out there – you want to find just one who's your soulmate and stick with him. You are confident in love – you aren't likely to be 'controlled' by a boy, even if you're really keen on him. You're not in a rush to make any long-term relationship decisions; you're too busy enjoying all other areas of life to tie yourself down. You are also not the kind of girl who would ever put a boy before her mates – you appreciate that your mates have been there before boys even appeared on the scene, and will be there for a long time to come.

★ *If you scored 21 to 29:*

You are most like Izzie. When you fall for a boy, you fall hard. There's always the danger that you can become obsessed with a boy and risk ignoring and upsetting your mates. With your outgoing personality and striking looks, you don't have a problem attracting boys – you just have a problem keeping them. Either you realise after the first few dates that the boy isn't quite as captivating as you thought he was, or you simply become bored with him and move on. Being dumped can plunge you into deep depression – but good mates will always help you bounce back.

### ★ *If you scored 30 to 38:*

You are most like Nesta. You never have a problem attracting boys – they're always falling at your feet. Your biggest trauma is how to pick and choose between them. You don't let yourself get swept away by relationships. Having fun times is just as important to you in dating as having romantic times. However, if that physical sparkle begins to die away, it's all over – out with the old and in with the new. After all, when it comes to boys, life is like a box of chocolates . . . lots of different types to try!

### ★ *If you scored 39 to 48:*

You are most like TJ. You can go for ages without seeing a boy you fancy and then one (or even two) comes along out of the blue who knocks you for six. When you meet someone you have chemistry with, it's always a very strong attraction. For you, it's not just physical. You find yourself attracted to a boy as much for his personality as for his buff bod. But if things go wrong, you're philosophical. What's meant to be is meant to be. You can put a relationship that's run its course behind you and look forward to when the next stomach-flipping, heart-stopping encounter hits you.

# Who are you most like ... overall?

Add up the points you have just scored in each one of the Section 1 quizzes, to find out which of the girls you are most like overall.

★ *If you scored 96 to 168:*
Fashionable and funky, fun and a fab friend, you are most like the joker of the pack, Lucy.

★ *If you scored 169 to 240:*
Wise and witty, intriguing, intuitive and inspirational, you are most like the mad, magical, mystical Izzie.

★ *If you scored 241 to 312:*
Classy and cool, delightful and delectable, you are most like star-to-be Nesta.

★ *If you scored 313 to 384:*
Streetwise and sassy, sporty and smart, you are most like TJ – the babe-with-brains.

# Quizzes from the Mates, Dates mob

Time to discover the real you with these personality quizzes from Lucy, Nesta, Izzie, TJ – and Tony.

# How good a mate are you? – by Lucy

Izzie, TJ, Nesta and I are the 'bestest' of best mates – and we want it to stay that way forever. But we're not just lucky. We work at it too. Being a good mate takes an effort – and keeps taking an effort. Like the saying on one of Mum's angel cards: if you want a friend, be a friend. Meaning if you take the time to care, in return, you'll have good mates. And that's the most important thing in the world.

Try my quiz to see just how good a mate you are. Don't forget to record your scores – add them up and you'll get your final rating from yours truly at the end. Love, Lucy xx

## 1. What would your best mate say is the best thing about your friendship?

★ We don't cramp each other's style            3

★ We have a right laugh together                2

★ We have the same taste in boys               1

★ We are there for each other through the bad times as well as the good            4

2.  **What would you do if you saw a new girl at school looking lonely in the playground?**

★  Go over and start up a conversation  2

★  Take my best mates over and introduce ourselves  3

★  Throw a party with the new girl as the guest of honour  4

★  Let her get on with things on her own – she'll find her feet in her own time  1

3.  **What would you give up for your best mate?**

★  My last Rolo  1
★  The comfiest chair in the café  2
★  My last fiver  3
★  The boy I've fancied for ages, because she likes him too  4

4.  **Your best mate moves far away. How do you plan to keep in touch?**

★  By phone or email every week – and I stick to it  3

★  By phone or email every day – and I stick to it  4

★  By phone or email as often as possible  2

★  I plan to keep in touch but am rubbish at sticking to plans  1

**5. What would you do if you saw your best mate's boyfriend sitting in a coffee bar with another girl, holding hands?**

★ Nothing – I would tell myself it's all above board and that there's a perfectly innocent explanation                                    3

★ Storm in and demand to know what he thinks he's playing at                              2

★ Tell my best mate what I've seen and leave it up to her to decide where to take it from there                              4

★ Tell my best mate I think her boyfriend is up to no good                                  1

**6. Your best mate is going through a bad time. What do you do?**

★ Take her out for the afternoon, sit her down in her fave café, treat her to a cappuccino and listen while she airs her woes        3

★ Keep out of her way until things improve and she cheers up again                          1

★ Make allowances for her moodiness at first but get fed up with it after a while            2

★ Plan a series of treats for her – a makeover sesh one night, a visit to the movies another, a surprise party one weekend . . .      4

63

7. **If you and your mate were going out for the evening and you both wanted to wear the same top, what would you do?**

★ Let her wear it, with good grace     4
★ Let her wear it, but sulk all night     3
★ Make a mutual decision that neither of us should wear it     2
★ Fight her for it     1

8. **How often have you put a boy before your best mate? (Be honest, now!)**

★ Frequently     1
★ Sometimes     2
★ Rarely     3
★ Never     4

9. **You and your friend fancy the same boy. So . . .**

★ Let battle commence     1
★ I'm not bothered – I always get what I want     2
★ I'm not bothered – we're both treating it as a joke     3
★ I'd back off – I wouldn't dream of risking our friendship over a boy     4

**10. You can't stand your best mate's boyfriend because you know he bad-mouths her behind her back. What do you do?**

★ Drop them both and spend time with your other mates instead      2

★ Tell her I'm worried that he may not be as nice as she thinks he is, and that I don't want to see her get hurt      4

★ Snog him and tell her, so she dumps him      1

★ Lie to her and say that I think he's lovely, to protect her feelings      3

**11. It's your best mate's birthday. What do you have planned?**

★ I've arranged a sleepover for her and all her closest mates with lots of pampering treats      4

★ We're going for a fun evening out together      2

★ I've bought her a card and a pressie, but I'm going out with my boyfriend      1

★ I've clubbed together with my other mates and bought her something special      3

## 12. Which of the following best sums up your attitude to friendship?

★ Friendships are OK, but relationships with boys are more important     1

★ A friend in need is a friend indeed     2

★ True friends never let you down     4

★ Friendship is a two-way street – you get out what you put in     3

# Scores

★ *If you scored 12 to 20:*

You want mates to be part of your life, but − sorry to say this − you have a selfish streak. When it comes to the crunch, you'll always put number one first. And as for boys − well! You'll drop your best mate like a hot potato when a boy you fancy comes along. All's fair in love and war, you may think − but I'm telling you, boys will come and go, and the between times can be very lonely. On the other hand, if you make good friends, they'll always be there for you. So here's my advice: friendship is a two-way street, and, as I said before, if you want a friend, be a friend. Amen. Or as Nesta says: Ah, men.

★ *If you scored 21 to 29:*

You're probably never stuck for company, because you're more likely to have a big group of mates rather than a few close ones. You can enjoy yourself with a wide variety of people in different situations, so if you find yourself somewhere new, you'll never be on your own for long. Your best times are spent hanging out in a gang, having fun . . . however, you're not so keen on getting stuck in to sort out someone's problems when the going gets tough. So a word of warning from your Agony Aunt Lucy – being a fair-weather friend is fun, but on the day when the rain comes pouring down on your own head, who will be there to bring the sunshine back out for you?

★ **If you scored 30 to 38:**
You're a great mate, and you enjoy being part of a close group. You're caring and considerate, and you'll be there for your mates through thick and thin. However, you're not afraid to have your own interests and hobbies and to stand on your own two feet either. You don't feel that you and your mates have to *be* each other to be close. You respect your mates' differences and you expect the same space from them. If your mates are as good at give-and-take as you, you'll be friends for life.

★ **If you scored 39 to 48:**
You're a devoted friend – and you're always ready to hold out the hand of friendship to someone new. You're always thinking about what you can do to help the people closest to you, and you don't hesitate to put your mates before yourself. You're loyal and reliable, and you won't let your mates down when they're going through trials and traumas. You'd rather be hanging out with your mates than doing anything else in the world – even if it's being a shoulder to cry on rather than going out partying.

Just be careful that you allow your mates space when they need it. You have a tendency to be over-keen sometimes and can get carried away with your passions and plans for your mates. This may leave people feeling overwhelmed and as if they need to withdraw from you, leaving you wondering why. You may also sometimes try so hard to please your mates that you're not true to yourself. Don't be afraid to express your own opinions and preferences – good mates will love you for it.

# Who is your perfect boy? - by Nesta

The girls got me to write this one, because they reckon I'm the expert when it comes to all things boy-related. I suppose it's true; my main interests are boys, fashion, movies and boys. And it's true that my main talent – besides acting, of course, sweetie luvvie dahling – is pulling boys. But I'm by no means an expert – there are far too many types of boys for that. There are tall, dark and handsome; lean, mean and muscular; blond and sunkissed; moody and mysterious; cute and winsome; mad, bad and dangerous to know. There are nice guys, cool dudes, gorgeous geeks, smart alecs and love rats. There are brainboxes, trainspotters, boy-scouts, poets and sports stars. There are intense and brooding, cheeky and chirpy, intellectual and intriguing, active and athletic, wild and eccentric . . . The list is endless.

So now it's your turn. Count up your scores and find out who I reckon your dream date is at the end.

Enjoy!
Nesta
xxx

## 1.  How important are a boy's looks to you?

★  I like boys who are good-looking in an unconventional, edgy way    4

★  I can be attracted to different-looking boys, as long as the boy has a fit bod and a nice face    2

★  Looking like a hero is great, but behaving like a hero is even more important    3

★  Get real – a boy can never be too good-looking, can he?    1

## 2.  Which of these qualities is most important to you in a boy?

★  Having shared interests and values    2

★  Being exciting, dare-devil and intriguing    4

★  A combination of charisma and rippling muscles    1

★  Being able to express his feelings    3

## 3.  Which of these qualities would instantly put you right off a boy?

★  Dirty fingernails    1

★  A cocky attitude    2

★  Being too serious and intense    4

★  Lying    3

**4.** **Which of these chat-up lines would work best on you?**

★ I feel like I know you – have we met somewhere before?     3

★ You have beautiful eyes     1

★ Have we ever dated? No? We should have done . . .     4

★ I can't believe you're here, I didn't know you liked jazz/football/Quentin Tarantino (fill in your fave interest as appropriate)     2

**5.** **How would you like your boyfriend to act when his friends are around?**

★ It's fine if he acts cool – I find cool attractive     4

★ I'd like him to be confident with me, holding my hand or putting his arm around me     1

★ I'd like him to act the same as when we're on our own together, to just be himself     2

★ I'd prefer him to get rid of his mates, because it's best when it's just him and me     3

**6.** **Would you rather go out with a boy who was really into . . .**

★ Sports, e.g. swimming, tennis and the gym     1

★ Artistic things, e.g. music concerts, art galleries and *Feng Shui*     3

★ Socialising, e.g. going to cafés, the movies and the shops                                        4

★ Intellectual things, e.g. science museums, historic houses and political organisations      2

**7. You're going out with a boy who has become really possessive. How do you feel about this?**

★ I am flattered – it means he's really into me      4

★ I expect it – I'm really possessive too      3

★ I put up with it to a certain extent, but then I tell him to get a grip and get over himself      2

★ I can't stand being told what I can and can't do, so I dump him      1

**8. How would your parents be most likely to describe your ideal boyfriend?**

★ A bit of a lad      4

★ A heart-throb      1

★ Seems like a very nice boy      2

★ An old romantic      3

## 9. Where would a boy take you on the perfect date?

★ An intimate, romantic evening meal for two    3

★ A wild and crazy fun-filled day out at a
theme park    4

★ A laid-back afternoon at the seaside with a
fish 'n' chip lunch on the beach    2

★ The perfect date would be a surprise    1

## 10. Which of the following would you prefer a boy to buy you for a birthday present?

★ Cool jewels that cost a bomb    1

★ A fluffy teddy bear that growls 'I love you'    3

★ Sexy underwear    4

★ Tickets for a concert by your fave band or
for a performance of your fave show    2

## 11. When would you feel comfortable if a boy said, 'I love you'?

★ On the first date     3
★ After a couple of months of dating     2
★ After about a year of dating     1
★ I'd never feel comfortable if a boy said, 'I love you'     4

## 12. Which of the following would be your ideal date?

★ Orlando Bloom     3
★ Johnny Depp     4
★ James Bond     1
★ Justin Timberlake     2

# Scores

★ *If you scored 12 to 20:*

Your perfect boy has got to look good – we're talking jaw-dropping, show-stopping good . . . almost as good as you, in fact. We're thinking serious boy-babes. Because it's all about the looks, your ideal guy is probably a sports fan – doing, rather than watching. He'll have a buff bod with rippling muscles – and the confidence to match. But you're not lacking in the confidence department either – even though girls swarm around the object of your affection, like bees round a honeypot, you rest assured he's only got eyes for you. You don't necessarily expect love – but you do expect manners, class, sophistication and romance . . . besides amazing snogging technique, *naturellement.* But your man had better watch out if he starts to try to tell you what you can and can't do – you'll drop him like a hot potato and move on to the next drop-dead-gorgeous guy that comes along. After all, so many men, so little time . . .

★ *If you scored 21 to 29:*

Your ideal boy is the boy-next-door, with an added dash of star quality. For your perfect partnership, think Homer and Marge. OK, maybe not exactly, but you get what I mean! You like a boy to look good, but as long as you both have a great time together, looks take a second place. You like a boy to be laid-back and relaxed – you want him to be himself so you can just be yourself too. One of your biggest turn-offs is a boy with a cocky attitude or a boy who is trying too hard. You expect companionship, consideration and respect – with bags of fun, loads of laughs and heaps of kisses and cuddles.

★ *If you scored 30 to 38:*

*Romeo, Romeo, wherefore art thou, Romeo?* You're after a dashing hero, a swashbuckling knight in shining armour, who'll express his love and longing in poetry and grand gestures before sweeping you off your feet and carrying you off into the sunset. For you, romance is all. You're searching for your soulmate – someone who is one hundred per cent honest and loyal, and with whom you feel the deepest spiritual connection. But watch out – you're so keen on the idea of falling in love that you can throw yourself into relationships head first and lose sight of everyone and everything else. And yonder that way, fair flaxen-haired maiden, tragedy oft lies . . . and a hey nonny no, polish mi goblet and so on.

★ *If you scored 39 to 48:*

Hmm. You like bad boys – rock stars and rebels, actors with attitude. You're after action and adventure – with a little bit of danger thrown in for the ride. You don't expect hearts and flowers or any of that cheesy romance stuff – you're far too chilled for that. You're excited by individuality, unconventionality, originality, and probably several other 'alities' I can't think of right now. You're fascinated by your daredevil fella's spark and spirit, and you're happy to follow his lead – just be careful he doesn't plunge you into seriously deep water.

# How in touch are you with your spiritual side? - by Izzie

I don't know why the girls call me 'the wise woman' – I don't know any of the answers to life and death and stuff. But I do spend *a-g-e-s* thinking about all the questions. Why are we here? Have we been here before? Why do bad things happen in the world? Is there anything beyond the world, out in space? Is there a God – or gods? Are there ghosts? Can they communicate with us and if they can walk through walls, why don't they fall through the floor? Is telepathy a real power? What happens when we die? Where do all the lost socks go? If we can buy coffee tables, why can't we buy decaffeinated coffee tables . . . ? All the biggies. If any of you lot can enlighten me, answers on a postcard *please*. In the meantime, have a go at my quiz and find out if you're a cosmic Cassandra or a down-to-earth Doris.

Peace, love, joy,
Izzie

### 1. What do you think of God?

★ I am very uncertain, but God is probably a
Force, like in *Star Wars*                                          3

★ I believe in God, and praying makes me
feel good                                                                        4

★ I don't believe in God at all                                    1

★ I haven't made my mind up, but I wonder
about it all quite a bit                                               2

### 2. How often do you find yourself thinking of someone at the same time as they suddenly ring you?

★ Always                                                                        4

★ Frequently                                3

★ Sometimes                                                                  2

★ Never                                                                           1

### 3. What do you understand by 'karma'?

★ Doesn't it have something to do with
past lives?                                                                     3

★ Karma – it's what you are when you take
some deep breaths and stop panicking                    2

★ It's the idea that what goes around, comes
around; as you sow, so shall you reap                     4

★ 'Karma Chameleon' – it was an Eighties song,
wasn't it? Or is it an Indian chicken dish:
chicken karma?                                                           1

**4. Which of these would you try in order to attract a boy you really fancy?**

★ Falling at his feet      1

★ Body language techniques, such as playing with my hair      2

★ Meditation and positive thinking, to boost my confidence and make myself more noticeable      4

★ A spell in which I write the boy's name seven times on a piece of paper and then carry it close to me for seven days and seven nights      3

**5. Which of these essential oils would you burn to make you feel uplifted and cheerful?**

★ Olive oil is the only oil I can think of – it's essential in the kitchen, does that count?      2

★ Lavender and rose      3

★ Jasmine and bergamot      4

★ I wouldn't burn any type of oil – it's a fire hazard      1

**6. How often do you read your horoscope?**

★ Always      4

★ Frequently      3

★ Sometimes      2

★ Never      1

**7. What would you think if you were walking along and you heard someone call out 'witch'?**

★ It is a compliment on my enchanting beauty and spellbinding personality   3

★ Someone is being rude to me, calling me a hag   2

★ I've overheard someone asking the question 'which?' about something totally unrelated to me   1

★ I'd take it as a compliment – I'm always hoping that my spells will work out   4

**8. What do you understand by 'aura'?**

★ It's short for aurora borealis (the Northern Lights) – we did it in geography   1

★ Isn't it something to do with the energy vibrations around your body?   3

★ Something to do with colours?   2

★ I had a photo of my aura taken at a psychic fair   4

**9. What type of music would you put on to feel chilled out and peaceful?**

★ *Chill Out Tunes From Ibiza*    2

★ An Enya album    3

★ I wouldn't put on any music – I'd rather watch the telly    1

★ A CD of whale and dolphin song    4

**10. What colour would you consider to be magical?**

★ Duh. Get a life.    1

★ Pink – like fairies and stuff    3

★ Purple    4

★ The colour of money    2

**11. Can you quote the Lord's Prayer?**

★ No, I'm Jewish/a Muslim/a Hindu/a Sikh/ a Buddhist, or of another religion    3

★ Doesn't it begin: 'Our Father, who art in Devon, Harold be thy name'? (Cue maniacal laughter)    2

★ Doesn't it begin: 'Our Father, who art in Heaven, hallowed be thy name'?    4

★ No, I can't . . . You gonna make somethin' of it?    1

## 12. **Do you believe in reincarnation?**

★ Definitely – I'm sure I've known some of
my family and mates before in past lives.
And reincarnation is making a come back.
Geddit?      4

★ No – when you die, you either go to heaven
or hell      3

★ I'm not sure – sometimes I have weird
feelings like I've been places or met people
before      2

★ What a load of rubbish – when you're dead,
you're dead      1

# Scores

★ *If you scored 12 to 20:*

You think religion is for saddos. If someone wanted to talk about your soul, you'd be more interested in a chat about the bottom of your shoes than about your spirit. You're in no doubt that there's nothing more to life than what you can see around you in the here and now, and death is simply *finito, nada, kaput* – for you, that's a cold, hard scientific fact. So, I ask you, how come some people have been hypnotised to have operations *without anaesthetic* and feel no pain? And how come some clairvoyants have helped guide police to the bodies of murder victims? And how come there really are machines that photograph someone's aura (the energy that surrounds their body)? . . . Hmmm? Got you thinking now, haven't I?!!!

★ *If you scored 21 to 29:*

You like to think of yourself as a spiritual person, but you're often on the wrong track. You probably think that Reiki is a Japanese martial art, that Hare Krishna is Henry Krishna's brother, and that 'incense' is spelled 'in-sense' and means 'fashion know-how'. You're sensitive to the mysteries of the universe –

you're probably intrigued by your dreams; you're
most likely superstitious; you may even think you've
seen a ghost or two – but you need to take much
more of an active interest in all-things cosmic, if you
want to really develop your spiritual side and realise
your full potential.

★ *If you scored 30 to 38:*
Spirituality is more important to you than it is to
most people, but you have developed the spiritual
side of yourself through your brain rather than
your senses. You feel more comfortable believing
in ancient wisdoms (such as organised religion,
witchcraft or numerology) than in trusting your
own unexplained experiences and feelings and
drawing your own conclusions. As a result, you may
leave yourself open to sometimes misinterpreting
spiritual guidance such as horoscopes and clairvoyant
messages. Perhaps you should follow the advice
Obi-Wan Kenobi once gave Luke Skywalker in
*Star Wars* – shut your eyes and trust in the Force . . .
or something like that. (Alternatively, my tip is to
try meditation – I've read that it can be good for
opening your third eye and giving you new spiritual
vision. I can't tell you that it definitely does though,
'cos I'm still working on it . . . )

★ *If you scored 39 to 48:*

Like me, you're fascinated by the spiritual side of life. You're sure you have a sixth sense just waiting to be awakened – if only you could find it. You've pondered religions, ancient and modern; you've opened your chakras; you've cleansed your aura, and you've channelled your chi. You still haven't found any answers, but you're going to stay searching, keeping your body and soul in tune with the universe through meditation and positive thought, healthy, organic eating and aromatherapy . . . but then you probably knew all that because no doubt you're somewhat psychic. Hope to meet you in this life – or the next.

# Are you a queen of the social scene? – by TJ

Supposedly I'm the most sorted and sensible one . . . maybe it's because of the wrinklies – I mean, my parents. They're much older than usual, and if you had to describe them in one word, it would be 'commonsense', or is that two words? See, sad isn't it, the things I ponder? Anyhow, maybe I've inherited it . . . or perhaps it rubs off at home, I don't know. The girls say that I'm living proof you can be sussed and savvy without being dull and boring. Hope so.
I think they mean that I know how to look after myself (and my mates) when I'm out and about, and that I'm cool in hairy social situations, such as knowing what knife and fork to use at posh dinners. To let you in on a secret, I never feel half as confident as I obviously look to everyone else – but carrying it off is half the battle, isn't it?

Anyway, see how you rate for social style.

Best of luck,
TJ xx

**1. You've been invited on a date that involves an activity you've never tried before, such as horse-riding. How do you react?**

★ I don't let myself get put off; I go along, and throw myself into it with gusto – let no one say I'm not a trier    3

★ I make sure I'm dressed right, so even if I'm rubbish at it, I look the part    2

★ I read up on the activity beforehand, so I don't make a total muppet of myself    4

★ I say no way, José – I'm not going to risk looking like a wombat    1

**2. What's your attitude towards smoking?**

★ I smoke because it makes me look sophisticated    1

★ I smoke to look cool, but I don't inhale    2

★ I refuse to smoke    3

★ I encourage other people to stop smoking    4

3. **What would you do if you want to go out with your mates, but find yourself short of cash?**

★ Do an extra shift at my part-time job     4
★ Stay in     1
★ Beg or borrow from my mates     2
★ Drum up some babysitting work     3

4. **Your best mate offers you a joint. What do you do?**

★ Take it – I do it all the time     1
★ Take it – but stub it out, so she can't smoke any more of it     4
★ Try it – but regret it and make up my mind not to do it again     2
★ Say no thanks – if she's really my mate she won't put pressure on me to try it     3

5. **What would you do if you walked past an old house of historic interest?**

★ Go in to look around and check out the artwork     4

★ Go in to sign something amusing in the guest book     2

★ Go in to see if there's a good café or souvenir shop     3

★ Go in to use the loo     1

**6. What should you do if you find yourself stranded somewhere with no dosh?**

★ Pretend I'm a street performer and earn some spare pennies     2

★ Pretend I'm a homeless person and beg for some spare pennies     1

★ Call someone from my mobile     4

★ I would have forgotten my mobile phone, so I'd get a cab to someone I know and ask them to pay the fare, saying I'll settle up later     3

**7. How do you feel about getting drunk as a skunk?**

★ Never, ever again     3

★ I do it all the time – I am Queen Skunk     1

★ I've never been really drunk     4

★ I don't mind getting a bit tipsy – I'm sure I can stay in control     2

8. **A boy you really like and you've been going out with for a while wants to sleep with you. You're not happy with the idea, but you think if you don't agree, he'll dump you. What do you do?**

★ Say no – if he dumps me, then it's his loss  4

★ Say no – and dump him before he dumps me  3

★ Say yes – I really like this boy and don't want to lose him  2

★ Say yes – I've been in this situation before and given in  1

9. **Do you think it's a good idea to walk along the street listening to your MP3 player on full blast?**

★ Yes – as long as I'm not singing out loud and making a prune of myself  2

★ Yes – as long as it's the latest model  1

★ No – I like to hear what's going on  3

★ No – because I won't hear if a mugger is coming up behind me, and also, if traffic's coming, I won't hear and might step off the kerb to cross the road and get knocked over  4

**10. Imagine you are in a bar or club. Which one of these statements is most important to you?**

★ It's OK to accept drinks from strangers because it saves me and my mates money    1

★ As long as me or a mate have bought my drink, it's OK to put it down, go off for a boogie and come back to it later    2

★ It's not OK for someone to drive if they've had just a couple of drinks    4

★ It's not a good idea to mix my drinks    3

**11. If you find yourself walking alone in a dark, secluded place, what should you do?**

★ Start running    2

★ Walk confidently with my head up, keep my mobile within reach but out of sight, not making eye-contact with strangers and heading for a populated area as soon as possible    3

★ Accept an offer of a lift    1

★ I'd always make sure that I wasn't walking alone in a dark, secluded place    4

## 12. What would you do after you've been to a dinner party?

★ Phone to say thank you      3

★ Send a text or email to say thank you      2

★ Post a card to say thank you      4

★ Burp and undo the button on my trousers      1

# Scores

★ *If you scored 12 to 20:*

Sigh. You've got a lot of growing up to do. Seriously, you need to wise up and smell the cappuccino on some serious safety issues. For instance, you should NEVER accept drinks from strangers, no matter how skint you are – you just can't tell what they may have laced them with. And you should never walk away from your drink and come back to it later for the same reason. On another note, it's never a good idea to mix your drinks because this can get you off your head really fast, without you even realising it. I'm not just saying this because no one wants to spend the evening with their head down the loo, but because, if you end up passed out cold somewhere, something truly horrific might happen to you. (Thank God for good mates – they'll always be there to take care of you . . . unless they're off their heads too, of course.) And lastly on booze-related issues, *never* get into someone's car if they've had a couple of drinks – just a small amount of alcohol can cloud a person's judgement when they're behind the wheel. You may feel foolish turning down a lift now, but you'll feel even more foolish if you wake up in a hospital bed. (Oh God,

I've become my mother! But it's true.) Last of last of all, if you find yourself walking alone in a dark, secluded place, never ever ever accept an offer of a lift from someone you don't absolutely trust. Got that? OK. Stay safe. (PS And if you think the right thing to do after a dinner party is to burp and undo the button on your trousers, you need serious help!)

★ *If you scored 21 to 29:*
I'm worried about you. You can be pressured into things just because everyone else is doing them, such as getting drunk, taking drugs, or sleeping with their boyfriend. Lucy's mum (who is a counsellor) would say that you probably suffer from low self-esteem, and you need to take some time to find out who you really are and what you really want, so you can stop pleasing other people all the time. You've also got a serious lack of social confidence and you're letting it really hold you back – such as not trying a new activity because you're afraid you'll look like a prune. Get life in proportion. Everyone looks foolish once in a while – learn to lighten up and laugh at yourself. At the same time, you also need to take a bit more responsibility for yourself in certain areas – you can't expect others to bail you out forever with offers of money or lifts. If you can find ways to stand on your own two feet more, you'll be more independent and enjoy your freedom more as a result. So take charge of yourself, girl, and go for it!

★ *If you scored 30 to 38:*

It's as if you've dressed up in the perfect designer dress and killer heels, got fabby hair and glam make-up, are dripping in diamanté sparkle, and then you slip on a banana skin when you're making your grand entrance! You're very nearly there when it comes to social know-how, but you can't help taking a tumble now and then. For instance, never forget your mobile phone when you go out – you never know when an emergency might arise and you might need it. One of your greatest social skills is your enthusiasm for trying out new situations and meeting new people, even if you're unsure of your-self. Just watch out that you don't try the 'wrong' new things – it's much better to accept an invitation to go surfing than an invitation to try drugs. Life is all about learning through mistakes – and we all make loads as we go along, don't we? The point is, when you make mistakes, you realise them and you have the ability to put yourself back on the right path. Ten out of ten for self-awareness, guts and verve – you're living life to the full.

★ *If you scored 39 to 48:*

Congratulations – you're seriously streetwise and you're sparkling with social style. You always act sensibly, and you're not afraid to stand out from the crowd if you feel you would be putting yourself at risk by going with the flow. You also try to act responsibly towards others – however, don't get put off if you can't stop your parents smoking or your friends getting into drink and drugs; you can only try your best, and then be there for them if they run into problems. You go to a lot of effort to have good manners – little gestures like taking the time to buy and post a thank you card can really bring a smile to someone's face and brighten up their day. There's no chance you'd try someone's pot-pourri as a snack or sip water from a finger bowl if you were feeling thirsty – you're far too cool for that. So get out there and enjoy yourself – you're a queen of the social scene.

# Are you a goddess girlfriend or a dating disaster? - by Tony Costello

Hi girls, you've finally reached the best bit of this book – the bit written by me, expert snogger and top North London female object of desire, Tony Costello. I'd love to meet you sometime . . . *(Oh shut up, you smarmy creep! They've read the books, they know what you're like and they're not falling for it – Nesta)* As I was saying, I'd love to meet you and give you a personal dating rating, but just in case our paths never cross, I've devised this quiz to do it for you.

Tony

1. **The god of love, Tony Costello, has asked you out on a date. What do you turn up with?**

★ Unwashed hair     1
★ My best outfit on     3
★ My best underwear on     4
★ My best mate     2

**2.  You're on a first date and conversation is drying up. What do you do?**

★  Say, 'So, do you come here often?'    2

★  Become a motor mouth and waffle on about anything and everything that comes into my head    3

★  Sit there smiling, feeling like a prat    1

★  Feed my date lines that get him going on his fave subject, e.g. what are his top three fave films?    4


**3.  Who should pay on a date?**

★  Always the boy    1

★  Always the person who's done the asking out  2

★  It's best to take turns    4

★  It's always best to split the bill    3


**4.  You're not sure whether your snogging technique is up to scratch. What do you do?**

★  Put my worries to the back of my mind and forget about them    1

★  Read up on snogging techniques in magazines    3

★ Practise on the back of my hand 2

★ Ask Tony Costello if he'll test me out, and
give me tuition if I need it 4

**5. What do you think 'I'll call you later'
means in boy-speak?**

★ I promise to telephone you later on 1

★ I may ring you in the next couple of days 2

★ I might ring you in a week or so 3

★ *Ciao bella*, you're history 4

**6. Which of these is the worst time to call
your boyfriend?**

★ Late at night, when his parents might
answer the phone 4

★ When a big footie match is on as he's bound
to be in 2

★ When his fave TV programme is on (ditto
as above) 1

★ When I know he's with a bunch of his mates 3

7. **You're going to dump your boyfriend (it's obviously not Tony Costello). Which way would you choose to do it?**

★ Get a friend to do it for me     2

★ By text, email, phone or letter     3

★ Explain why in person     4

★ Stand him up and hope he gets the message     1

8. **You've got fed up with waiting for the object of your affection to ask you out, so you've plucked up the courage to ask him instead. He says no. How do you react?**

★ I burst into hysterical weeping and run off     1

★ I smile calmly and say, 'Well, you'll never know what you're missing then'     3

★ I spread rumours all round school that he's gay     2

★ I say, 'What about your gorgeous mate then?'     4

9. **Your boyfriend is ill in bed with the man flu. What do you do?**

★ Go out with my mates until he's recovered     2

★ Visit every day after school and do all the homework he's falling behind on     4

★ Visit every couple of days and make sympathetic noises but go away before he gets irritated     3

★ Turn up every day after school and moan about why doesn't he feel like snogging me    1

## 10. What is the worst thing to do on a date?

★ Be very late    2
★ Ask questions like, 'Are you a virgin?'    3
★ Pick your nose    1
★ Chat up the waiter    4

## 11. The object of your affection (who else but Tony Costello?) is about to snog you. What do you do?

★ Relax    4
★ Remove or swallow my chewing gum    3
★ Run to the loo and clean my teeth    2
★ Wish I hadn't had curry for dinner    1

## 12. Which of the following would be your top romantic place?

★ A funky old café with big sofas    2
★ Anywhere candlelit    1
★ The local park on a summer's night    3
★ Tony Costello's bedroom    4

# Scores

★ *If you scored 12 to 20:*

OK, there's no easy way to say this. When it comes to dating, you're a boy's worst nightmare. You may look babelicious, but when you're out on a date you behave like Sandra Bullock in *Miss Congeniality* – BEFORE the makeover. Here are Tony Costello's *Ten Commandments for Relationship Success*, to give you a few essential pointers:

1) Thou shalt always wash thy hair before a date, that is if thou wilt stand any hope of having thy tresses tousled and caressed.

2) Thou shalt never bring thy best mate along on a date unannounced.

3) Thou shalt not expect a decent phone conversation if thou telephonest thy boyfriend when his fave telly programme or a big footie match is on.

4) Thou shalt not expect any sort of conversation if thou telephonest thy boyfriend when thou knowest he is with a bunch of his mates or when thou knowest his parents are bound to answer the phone.

5) Thou shalt never have curry, chilli, onions (or any other pungent food) immediately before a date, if thou wilt stand any hope of being snogged.

6) Thou shalt never moan if thy boyfriend is ill and doesn't want to get cuddly. It is thy duty to mop his brow and attend to his every need, not to make selfish, girly demands.

7) Thou shalt never be very late for a date and leave thy boyfriend looking like a prat.

8) Thou shalt never pick thy nose on a date and leave thyself looking like a prat.

9) Thou shalt always offer to pay thy way or thou shalt look mighty stingy.

10) Thou shalt never, ever, chat up the waiter. This is a mortal sin.

★ *If you scored 21 to 29:*

You're much more comfortable going out with your mates than with a boy. In fact, you've probably got your best mate to ask a boy out for you – or even worse, to dump a boy for you. Let me reassure you, on the contrary to what girls think, boys are not a totally alien species. *(Er… in your own strange alien language, dear bro, thou speakest out thy bottom here – Nesta.)* Basically, you should behave towards a boy just the same as you would towards your mates. For instance, if you wouldn't be late to meet a mate, don't be late to meet a boy. If you wouldn't blush and get stuck for something to say when talking to a mate, why blush and get stuck when talking to a boy? If you wouldn't moan when one of your mates felt ill and couldn't go out with you, why moan when a boy feels ill and can't go out with you?

*(For sooth and strike me down, he maketh a point for once – Nesta.)* Thank you. So stop being such a giggling girly-girl, and dating will soon become a dream, not a disaster.

### ★ *If you scored 30 to 38:*

Any boy would be lucky to go out on a date with you – you know what's embarrassing and how to avoid it; you'd be good company, and you're up for romance if the chemistry's right. BUT (could you see that coming?) you can sometimes be rather intense. And I'll give you Tony's top tip – boys HATE to feel that they're being put under the microscope, having demands made of them, or pressurised into something 'serious' before they're ready. So my advice to you is: be cool, relax, and before you know it you'll have the cream of boykind flocking around you.

### ★ *If you scored 39 to 48:*

You're obviously God's gift to mankind and we're made for each other. Where do you live? I'm coming round . . .

# SECTION 3

## So you think you know Mates, Dates?

Feel as if you know the books off
by heart? Check out these quizzes and find
out how much you really remember!

# 1

# Easy-peasy-lemon-squeezy level

Here are some super-simple starter questions on all your favourite *Mates, Dates* characters and events, just to get you going. Have fun . . .

**1. Which two girls have known each other the longest (since junior school)?**

a) Lucy and Izzie
b) Nesta and TJ
c) TJ and Lucy
d) Izzie and Nesta

**2. What do the initials 'TJ' stand for in TJ's name?**

a) Tracy Joanne
b) Theresa Joanne
c) Tracy Jayne
d) Theresa Jayne

3. **What is the name of the slimming club Izzie goes to?**

a) Watch Your Weight
b) Slim Fit
c) Weight Winners
d) Figure Fighters

4. **What does TJ call the language she comes out with when she is taken over by Noola?**

a) Alienbabespeak
b) Cyberlingo
c) Outerringroadmadness
d) Outerspaceagongalese

5. **Lucy is conscious of being flat-chested. What nickname do her brothers sometimes call her?**

a) Vera the Vest-Wearer
b) Penelope Pancake
c) Nancy No Tits
d) Barbara Braless

6. **What does Lucy's dad call the Hollywood Bowl in Finchley?**

a) Teen Paradise
b) A ridiculous waste of money
c) Teen Heaven
d) A parent's nightmare

**7.    What is Lucy's mum's job?**

a)    She is a beautician
b)    She is a teacher
c)    She is an accountant
d)    She is a counsellor

**8.    What is Nesta's favourite make and flavour of ice cream?**

a)    Häagen-Dazs Cookies and Cream
b)    Häagen-Dazs Pecan
c)    Ben & Jerry's Phish Food
d)    Ben & Jerry's Chunky Monkey

**9.    What is Nesta's mum's job?**

a)    She is a journalist
b)    She is a newsreader
c)    She is an interior designer
d)    She is a fashion designer

**10.   What are Izzie's two favourite essential oil scents?**

a)    Neroli and bergamot
b)    Peppermint and rosemary
c)    Ylang-ylang and patchouli
d)    Rose and jasmine

## 11. Which boy gave Lucy her very first kiss?

a) William Lewis
b) Luke De Biasi
c) Tony Costello
d) Teddy Ambrosini Junior

## 12. What was the name of the boy who gave TJ her first snog?

a) Scott Harris
b) Luke De Biasi
c) Lal Lovering
d) Steve Lovering

## 13. What is the name of the model Nesta persuaded to come to the Diamond Destiny charity dance and fashion show?

a) Jewel Jackson
b) Scarlett Kornikova
c) Lila Hackett
d) Star Axford

## 14. What is the name of TJ's pet dog?

a) Coco
b) Mojo
c) Toto
d) Hobo

**15. What are the names of Lucy's two dogs?**

a) Bill and Ben
b) Robbie and Justin
c) Ben and Jerry
d) Ant and Dec

**16. What type of dogs are Lucy's two pets?**

a) Fat Labradors
b) Scruffy Westies
c) Drooly Boxers
d) Pampered Poodles

**17. When Lucy's two dogs were puppies they ate their way through a whole tub of ice cream. What flavour was it?**

a) Ben & Jerry's Cherry Garcia
b) Häagen-Dazs Caramel Truffle
c) Ben & Jerry's Chunky Monkey
d) Häagen-Dazs Strawberry Cheesecake

**18. What is the name of the band Izzie sometimes sings with?**

a) Prince Naseem
b) Lady Marmalade
c) Count Basie
d) King Noz

**19. What is the name of the lead singer in the band Izzie sometimes sings with?**

a) Ben
b) Sam
c) Dan
d) Tom

**20. What is Izzie's dad's job?**

a) He owns a health food shop
b) He is a lecturer in English Literature
c) He is a research scientist at a university
d) He is a piano teacher

**21. Who is Star Axford's father?**

a) Jon Axford, the movie star
b) Zac Axford, the rock star
c) Jack Axford, the film director
d) Frank Axford, the jazz singer

**22. What is the name of Star Axford's brother?**

a) Ollie Axford
b) Otis Axford
c) Ethan Axford
d) Hugh Axford

**23. What is the name of the Camden clothing shop Ben works in?**

a)  Rockville
b)  Techno-Mutants R Us
c)  Cyberdog
d)  Cheap 'n' Cheerful

**24. What champagne cocktail did Nesta get drunk on when Izzie first sang with her band in concert?**

a)  Kir Royale
b)  Buck's Fizz
c)  Bellini
d)  Disco Fizz

**25. What is the name of the boy Izzie fell for who worked on a stall at Camden Market?**

a)  Mick
b)  Mike
c)  Mack
d)  Mark

**26. What is the name of the boy Nesta fell for who took her horse-riding?**

a)  Steven Perkins-Lloyd
b)  Simon Peddington-Lee
c)  Samuel Parker-Lewis
d)  Simon Potterton-Lang

**27. When Nesta went horse-riding for the very first time, what was the name of the horse she rode?**

a) Sally
b) Smedley
c) Hedley
d) Heddie

**28. What doggy-sounding nickname does Nesta give posh girl Tanya and her horrible friend, Cressida Dudley-Smythe?**

a) The Pedigree Chums
b) The Pedigree Pals
c) The Pedigree Mates
d) The Pedigree Mutts

**29. Who once dyed their hair bright green for a family wedding, to match their bridesmaid's dress?**

a) Izzie
b) Lal Lovering
c) Nesta
d) Lucy

## 30. What is painted on the boot of Lucy's parents' turquoise Volkswagen Beetle?

a) A big bright daisy
b) A big silver star
c) A big lilac flower
d) A big red heart

*Now check the answers on page 156.*

# Scores

★ *If you scored 1 to 10:*
Are you sure you've read the *Mates, Dates* books?
You've obviously eaten so much Ben & Jerry's that
it's frozen your brain. You'll have to mug up a bit if
you want to think of yourself as a true mate of
Nesta, Lucy, Izzie and TJ – so pick up those books
and refresh your memory . . .

★ *If you scored 11 to 20:*
Not bad – but could do better. Were you distracted
by a snogsome boy or two while you were answering
the questions? Before you try Level 2, put a drop or
two of rosemary oil in your aromatherapy burner to
keep yourself sharp and focused . . .

★ *If you scored 21 to 30:*
Well done! You certainly know your Lal Loverings
from your Luke De Biasis, and your Bellini from
your baloney. Have a cappuccino and a big slice of
four-cheese pizza to celebrate your success.

# 2

# One-of-the-gang level

Call yourself a *Mates, Dates* fan? This quiz will really put you to the test. So just how well do you *really* know Lucy, Izzie, Nesta and TJ?

**1.    What are the names of the four boys in King Noz?**

a)    Ben, Mike, Eddy, Boz
b)    Ben, Mark, Elliot, Biff
c)    Ben, Micky, Eric, Baz
d)    Ben, Martin, Elliot, Abs

**2.    Where do King Noz rehearse?**

a)    Ben's bedroom, done out like a space capsule
b)    Ben's garage, done out like an Arabian tent
c)    Ben's garden shed, done out like a recording studio
d)    Ben's friend's garage, done out like a Mongolian yurt

### 3. What do TJ's parents do for a living?

a) They are both teachers
b) They are both solicitors
c) They are both artists
d) They are both doctors

### 4. How much money did rock star Zac Axford donate at the Diamond Destiny Dance?

a) £35,000
b) £40,000
c) £45,000
d) £50,000

### 5. What was the name of the girl at Lucy, Izzie, Nesta and TJ's school who accidentally got pregnant?

a) Candice Carter
b) Candice Cartwright
c) Candice Carmichael
d) Candice Carpenter

### 6. What was the name of the boyfriend of the girl who got pregnant?

a) Ellis
b) Etienne
c) Elias
d) Elliot

**7. What school did this boyfriend go to?**

a) Archway Comprehensive
b) Finsbury Park Secondary
c) Wood Green High
d) Islington Grammar

**8. What is the name of the boy who lives next door to TJ, whom TJ used to have a crush on?**

a) Steven Henry
b) Scott Harris
c) Simon Harrington
d) Stuart Hawkes

**9. How long did TJ take to beat Lucy's brother Steve at arm-wrestling?**

a) Two seconds
b) Five seconds
c) Ten seconds
d) Twenty seconds

**10. How long did TJ take to beat Lucy's brother Lal at arm-wrestling?**

a) Two seconds
b) Five seconds
c) Ten seconds
d) Twenty seconds

**11. What ethnic mix is Nesta?**

a) Half Jamaican, half Spanish, with a bit of Italian thrown in

b) Half Jamaican, half Brazilian, with a bit of Portugese thrown in

c) Half Jamaican, half Greek, with a bit of Italian thrown in

d) Half Jamaican, half Italian, with a bit of Spanish thrown in

**12. When Nesta couldn't prick her finger to become blood-sisters with Lucy, Izzie and TJ, what type of crisp did she suggest they bond over instead?**

a) A Hula Hoop

b) A Quaver

c) A Frazzle

d) A Pringle

**13. What was the name of the cocktail book Izzie made cocktails from at Nesta's house, getting seriously drunk in the process?**

a) *Cocktails for City Nights*

b) *Cocktails for City All-Nighters*

c) *Cocktails – Shaken Not Stirred*

d) *Cosmopolitan Cocktails*

## 14. What was the name of the boy Izzie initially thought of as 'Park Boy'?

a) Jason Harper
b) Josh Harper
c) Josh Harrington
d) Jake Harman

## 15. What are the only type of earrings Izzie's mum will wear?

a) Little pearl studs
b) Little diamond studs
c) Small gold hoops
d) Diamanté danglers

## 16. What is the name of Ollie Axford's girlfriend in Cornwall?

a) Caitlin McKenzie
b) Katie Campbell
c) Cleo Kyriakos
d) Cat Kennedy

## 17. What is the name of Ollie Axford's non-famous sister?

a) Mia
b) Pia
c) Lia
d) Tia

**18. What is the name of Ollie Axford's family home in Cornwall?**

a)  Baxter Place
b)  Bennett Mansions
c)  Barton Hall
d)  Bembroke Lodge

**19. What was the name of the holiday home TJ and her family went to stay in on the Rame Peninsula, Cornwall?**

a)  Rose Harbour Cottage
b)  Seaview Heights
c)  Lilac Cottage
d)  The Old Dairy

**20. What was the name of the new TV teenage discussion show launched by one of Nesta's dad's friends?**

a)  *Hot Stuff*
b)  *Teen Talk*
c)  *Big Ideas*
d)  *Talking Heads*

**21.** **The guest on the first of the TV teenage discussion shows was to be Alicia Prowdy – what was she famous as?**

a)   An American singer–songwriter
b)   An American movie star
c)   An Australian soap star
d)   A Canadian gymnast

**22.** **What was the name of the boy Izzie met while he was doing work experience on the TV teenage discussion show?**

a)   Leonardo
b)   Raphael
c)   Sebastian
d)   Gabriel

**23.** **What was the name of the ballet Nesta had seen Eleanor Lewis in, before Eleanor became ill with bone cancer?**

a)   *The Sleeping Beauty*
b)   *The Snow Queen*
c)   *The Nutcracker*
d)   *The Ice Maiden*

### 24. What nickname does Izzie give her two stepsisters?

a) The Sisters from Hell
b) The Blister Sisters
c) The Ugly Sisters
d) The Sisters of Doom

### 25. What are the names of Izzie's two stepsisters?

a) Griselda and Heidi
b) Claudia and Amelia
c) Clarice and Emily
d) Gertrude and Helga

### 26. What are Izzie's two stepsisters' jobs?

a) They are both solicitors
b) They are both bank managers
c) They are both lifeguards
d) They are both accountants

### 27. What is the name of Luke De Biasi's sister?

a) Marisa
b) Marie
c) Mariella
d) Marina

**28. What was the name of the celebrity journalist who visited the girls' school and called TJ 'Lara Croft'?**

a)   Dan Samuels
b)   Den Hammond
c)   Sam Denham
d)   Sam Simmonds

**29. What is the name of the hairdressing academy where Lucy was given a disastrous haircut on trainee night?**

a)   The Auden Academy
b)   The Aurora School
c)   The Audrey School
d)   The Aura School

**30. Izzie had a henna tattoo done at a Mind, Body and Spirit fair at Alexandra Palace. What was the design and where on her body did she have it painted?**

a)   A chain of stars around her wrist
b)   A delicate bracelet of leaves around her ankle
c)   A Celtic bracelet around her upper arm
d)   A butterfly at the base of her spine

*Time to fast-forward to page 156 to see how you got on.*

# Scores

★ *If you scored 1 to 10:*

Not bad, not bad at all. Lucy says, as a reward for your efforts, you should treat yourself to a relaxing bubble bath and a pampering face pack. Enjoy.

★ *If you scored 11 to 20:*

Seriously impressive. Izzie says that you deserve at least a family-sized bar of delicious organic Green & Blacks' chocolate – all to yourself. In one sitting.

★ *If you scored 21 to 30:*

Ooooooh, you're definitely a babe-with-brains, like TJ. In fact, TJ wants to know where you hang out. She'd like to meet you.

# Friends-forever level

Prepare yourself for a seriously tough grilling on all the most in-depth *Mates, Dates* inside info. Consider yourself truly one of the girls? Get ready to find out . . .

**1. When Ollie Axford asked TJ out, why did she say she couldn't go?**

a) She wanted to go to a cinema in Camden to see a special double-bill of classic Marlon Brando movies

b) She wanted to go up to a bookshop in Muswell Hill to hear one of her favourite authors, Leila Ferrin, giving a talk

c) She wanted to go to the ice rink at Alexandra Palace to watch an ice hockey match

d) She wanted to go to Highgate Cemetery to begin a guided 'Ghost Walk around North London'

**2.** **What was the name of the tattooist who did Lucy and Izzie's belly-button piercing?**

a) Dave
b) Dirk
c) Doug
d) Del

**3.** **What is the name of the girl who co-edits the school magazine with TJ?**

a) Emma Ford
b) Emily Floyd
c) Francesca Foakes
d) Erica Francis

**4.** **What was the name of the school news-letter before TJ changed it to *For Real*?**

a) *The Real Deal*
b) *Free School News*
c) *Freemont News*
d) *School Reality*

**5.** **What is the name of Izzie's mum's cleaning lady?**

a) Mrs Dawson
b) Mrs Lawson
c) Mrs Sampson
d) Mrs Mason

6. **How much weight did Izzie put on over Christmas, New Year and the school trip to Florence?**

a) Eight pounds
b) Ten pounds
c) Twelve pounds
d) Fourteen pounds (a stone)

7. **Who were the two teachers who supervised the school trip to Florence?**

a) Mr Jackson and Mrs Ellis
b) Mrs Jackson and Mr Ellis
c) Mrs Johnson and Mr Elwes
d) Mr Johnson and Mrs Elwes

8. **What was the name of the American boy Lucy met in Florence?**

a) Theo Constantinedes the Third
b) Teddy Ambrosini Junior
c) Thomas Walker Forte
d) Teddy Harold Hilton

9. **What are the names of the American boy's two stepsisters?**

a) Alicia and Catherine
b) Amanda and Cecily
c) Arianna and Cecilia
d) Ashley and Corinne

**10. Where was the American boy staying in Florence?**

a) Hotel Villa Corelli
b) Hotel Palazzo Pitti
c) Hotel Una Vittoria
d) Hotel Holiday Inn

**11. What was the name of the old lady who left Lucy's brother, Lal, £50,000 in her will, because he had been kind to her cat?**

a) Mrs Gruber
b) Mrs Huber
c) Mrs Goldberg
d) Mrs Finkelstein

**12. What is the only thing that TJ's sister, Marie, is any good at cooking?**

a) Chilli con carne
b) Lasagne
c) Spaghetti Bolognese
d) Moussaka

**13. What was the name of the hotel where TJ's sister, Marie, got married?**

a) Coney Island Hotel
b) Burgh Island Hotel
c) The Isle of Wight Hotel
d) The Islets of Langerhans Hotel

**14. Besides TJ and Luke De Biasi, who worked on the 'inhabitants and historical houses in North London' project?**

a) Candice Carter and Michaela Wilcox
b) Sian Collins and Olivia Jacobs
c) Ashia Hussein and Harriet Parkes
d) Erin Brookes and Chantelle Bryce

**15. What was the name of the boy Lucy met at the relaxation workshop weekend in Devon?**

a) Daniel
b) Dylan
c) Derek
d) Damian

**16. What nickname did the boy at the relaxation workshop weekend give Lucy?**

a) Snuggle Bunny
b) Cuddle Bug
c) Little Ted
d) Little Bear

**17. What was the name of the hotel Izzie and her mother went to stay in during the relaxation workshop weekend in Devon?**

a)   Montague Towers
b)   Montmorency House
c)   Montbury Lodge
d)   Mont St Michel Hotel

**18. What was the name of the dog TJ's dad had when he was a child?**

a)   Fang
b)   Wolfie
c)   Rex
d)   Roy

**19. What body part is school bully Wendy Roberts missing?**

a)   She has no hair and wears a wig
b)   She has dentures instead of her two front teeth
c)   She is missing the tip of her little finger on her left hand
d)   She is missing her right earlobe

**20. What was the name of the film TJ went to see with Scott Harris?**

a) *Alien Mutants in Cyberspace*
b) *Attack of the WereBabes*
c) *Vampire Invasion of Venus*
d) *There's a Rhino Loose in the City*

**21. Why did Candice Carter tell Miss Watkins at school that she wanted to be a lifeguard when she grew up?**

a) So she could look good in shorts
b) So she could get a suntan working at outdoor pools in the summer
c) So she could be like Pamela Anderson in *Baywatch*
d) So she could give all the boys the kiss of life

**22. What is the name of the school Nesta's brother, Tony, goes to?**

a) St Peter's
b) St Michael's
c) St Luke's
d) St Paul's

**23. What is the name of the man to whom Izzie's stepsister, Amelia, got married?**

a) Justin
b) Jasper
c) Jeremy
d) James

**24. What was the shape of the cake at Izzie's stepsister's wedding?**

a) A vintage car
b) A champagne bottle
c) A stiletto shoe
d) A calculator

**25. When Izzie was studying Hinduism at school, she made a badge saying what?**

a) Be kind to spiders – unless you want to be one in the next life
b) Reincarnation's making a comeback
c) The cobra will bite you, whatever you call it
d) Call on the gods, but row away from the rocks

**26. Nesta has an uncle whose surname is Spielberg. What is his first name?**

a) Steven
b) Leister
c) Walter
d) Oscar

**27. When Nesta phoned the Morgan Elliot model agency, to enquire about part-time work, how much money – in total – did they say she would need to get started?**

a) £260
b) £300
c) £330
d) £360

**28. What is the name of Lucy's favourite teddy, which she's had since she was five?**

a) Mr Maguire
b) Mr Magoo
c) Mr Mackety
d) Mr Mackenzie

**29. How many sub-personalities does TJ reckon she has?**

a) Two
b) Four
c) Six
d) Eight

**30. Name them!**

*Now check out the answers on page 157.*

# Scores

★ *If you scored 1 to 10:*

Great work – these questions are even tougher than trying to persuade Star Axford to appear at the Diamond Destiny Dance. You are the winner of the title '*Mates, Dates* Brainbox – Third Class'. Be proud. Be very proud.

★ *If you scored 11 to 20:*

Give yourself three cheers and practise your best smug smirk – when Izzie tried this quiz, she scored only 19, so you're in pretty good company. Award yourself the distinguished honour of '*Mates, Dates* Brainbox – Second Class'.

★ *If you scored 21 to 30:*

Heap big congratulations – you're definitely one of the gang. Nesta, Lucy, Izzie and TJ salute you! You are the venerable recipient of the rarely awarded prize – '*Mates, Dates* Brainbox – First Class'.

★  *If you scored 31 to 37:*

Are you sure you didn't cheat? . . . Hmmm . . . Well, in any case, top marks for ingenuity and dedication! Consider yourself deserving of the ultimate title – '*Mates, Dates* Brainbox – First Class With Honours'.

(Sorry, no badges – just the reputation and the prestige. But Lucy says you could always make yourself one . . .)

# Mad match-ups and mini-quizzes

Just a bit of a laugh...

# Lucy's T-shirt slogans

**Match the beginning and ends of these wise sayings.**

*Beginnings:*

Princess, having had enough of princes, . . .

God made us sisters, . . .

Your village phoned. . . .

Absence makes the heart grow fonder . . .

Warning! . . .

I can see clearly now . . .

Out of my mind . . .

Fashion . . .

When God made boys . . .

Falling in love is awfully simple. . . .

A woman needs a man like . . .

The perfect boy? . . .

Insanity is hereditary. . . .

As ye smoke, . . .

*Endings:*

. . . Falling out of love is simply awful.

. . . my brain has gone.

. . . – back in 5 minutes.

. . . They want their idiot back.

. . . seeks frog.

. . . a fish needs a bicycle.

. . . so shall ye reek.

. . . she was only joking.

. . . (of somebody else).

. . . You get it from your kids.

. . . Next mood swing in 5 minutes.

. . . Police Academy.

. . . chocolate made us friends.

. . . One who snogs for half an hour and then turns into a pizza.

*Answers on page 158.*

143

# TJ's made-up books by made-up authors

**Can you match up each book title with the correct author?**

*Titles:*

*Modern Giants*

*Pain in the Neck*

*Over the Cliff*

*The Cat's Revenge*

*Rusty Bedsprings*

*Chicken Dishes*

*Bubbles in the Bath*

*A Stitch in Time*

*Chest Pain Remedies*

*Poo on the Wall*

*Dog Bites*

*Rhythm of the Night*

*Bad Falls*

*Chest Complaints*

*Run to the Loo*

*Body Parts*

*Authors:*

Nora Drumstick

Willie Makeit

Lauren Gitis

Hugh Mungous

Mark Time

R Stornaway

Justin Case

Hoo Flung Dung

Hugo First

Claude Bottom

I P Nightly

Ivor Windybottom

I Coffedalot

Ivor Tickliecoff

Anne Atomy

Eileen Dover

*Answers on page 158.*

# Lucy's mum's angel cards

## Can you match up the beginning of each angel card saying with the correct ending?

**Beginnings:**

The darkest hour . . .

Choice, not chance . . .

The tragedy in life doesn't lie in not reaching your goal. . . .

Don't wait for your ship to come in. . . .

The people who get on in the world are the people who get up and look for the circumstances they want. . . .

If you want a friend, . . .

No one can make you feel inferior . . .

**Endings:**

. . . determines destiny.

. . . be a friend.

. . . And if they can't find them, make them.

. . . without your permission.

. . . is just before dawn.

. . . Swim out to it.

. . . The tragedy lies in having no goal.

*Answers on page 159.*

# Parent-speak

**Parents don't always say what they mean. Can you match up these choice examples of parent-speak with the true meanings?**

*What they say:*

What's this lying on the floor?

I need to have a word.

That TV programme doesn't look very interesting.

It's getting late.

Your room's a mess.

Are you watching this TV programme?

It's time you learned how to look after yourself as I won't be around forever.

We need to talk.

You must learn to communicate.

Go ahead *(with raised eyebrow)*.

*What they mean:*

You've done something wrong.

Tidy it RIGHT NOW.

Wash up.

This is yours. Pick it up!

I'm going to tell you off.

Make my day!

You must learn to agree with me.

Turn it off.

I want to watch something else.

Go to bed.

*Answers on page 160.*

# Boy-speak

**Are you an expert at interpreting what boys say? Look at these examples of boy-speak and see if you can match them up with our translations.**

| *What they say:* | *What they mean:* |
| --- | --- |
| I need space. | I already am. |
| Let's just see how it goes. | I like my own way. |
| Would you like a back rub? | Back off, I'm feeling pressured. |
| Isn't it warm in here? | You're history, baby. |
| Hi. Your friend looks nice. | At least, not with you. |
| Don't get heavy. | She didn't fancy me. |
| She's ugly/a lesbian. | I want to grope you. |
| I'm not ready for a relationship. | I fancy her and I'm using you to get to her. |
| I'm very independent. | For my other girlfriends. |
| I think we should be free to date other people. | I don't feel the same about you. |
| We can still be friends. | I want to grope you and am hoping you'll take your clothes off. |

*Answers on page 161.*

# Anagrams – The girls

**Can you unravel these anagrams to make the names of ten girl characters in the *Mates, Dates* books?**

1. Cruel Long Ivy

2. Man Will Siesta

3. Anteater Nosh Jaw Set

4. Size Zero Fit

5. Recent Cardiac

6. Fart Rod Sax

7. Decent Yank

8. Radio Flax

9. Independent Goat Lay

10. Hey Scum Try Sidesaddle

*Answers on page 162.*

# Anagrams – The boys

**Unscramble these anagrams to make the names of ten boy characters in the *Mates, Dates* books.**

1.  Snooty Tolcel

2.  Evil Roll Nag

3.  Evolve Sir Gent

4.  Use Bike Dial

5.  Fried Lax Loo

6.  Limestone Den Dog Nip

7.  Shop Her Jar

8.  Slim Wail Wile

9.  Bridesmaid Run Into Joy

10. Rich Toss Rat

*Answers on page 162.*

# Order, order!

## Put the following books in the correct order that they come in the series:

Mates, Dates and Mad Mistakes

Mates, Dates and Portobello Princesses

Mates, Dates and Sizzling Summers

Mates, Dates and Diamond Destiny

Mates, Dates and Great Escapes

Mates, Dates and Sole Survivors

Mates, Dates and Inflatable Bras

Mates, Dates and Cosmic Kisses

Mates, Dates and Chocolate Cheats

Mates, Dates and Tempting Trouble

Mates, Dates and Sleepover Secrets

Mates, Dates and Pulling Power

*Answers on page 162.*

# Names and star signs

**The girls' first names and surnames have got muddled. Can you sort them out?**

1. TJ Williams

2. Nesta Foster

3. Izzie Lovering

4. Lucy Watts

**What sign of the zodiac is:**

5. Izzie?

6. Lucy?

7. Nesta?

8. TJ?

*Answers on page 163.*

# True or false?
# The parents

**Are these statements about
the *Mates, Dates* parents true or false?**

1.  Nesta's dad drives a Mercedes.

2.  TJ's best mate Hannah nicknamed TJ's dad
    'Sad Dad'.

3.  Izzie's stepmum is called Anna.

4.  Lucy's dad teaches the piano.

5.  Nesta's mum's usual perfume is Ô de Lancôme.

*Answers on page 163.*

# True or false? London

## Are these statements about *Mates, Dates* London true or false?

1. Lucy and TJ's favourite café, Raj's, is in Muswell Hill.

2. Camden Lock and Portobello Road are both sites of famous London markets.

3. The plush, old-fashioned Hampstead cinema Luke took TJ to was called the Everyday cinema.

4. Nesta's favourite curry house in Muswell Hill is called Ruby in the Dust.

5. People have been horseriding in Hyde Park in central London for three hundred years.

*Answers on page 163.*

# True or false?
# The boys

### Are these statements about
### the *Mates, Dates* boys true or false?

1. TJ's one-time boyfriend, Ollie Axford, has emerald-green eyes.

2. Gabriel, Izzie's would-be love interest, turned out to have a boyfriend called Adrian.

3. Daniel, the boy Lucy met at the relaxation workshop in Devon, wanted to go to the London School of Fashion after leaving school.

4. Fanciable celebrity journalist, Sam Denham, visited the girls' school on a motorbike.

5. Nesta's hook-up, William Lewis, is a red-head.

*Answers on page 164.*

# Answers

The moment of truth!
How did you get on?

# Answers

## ★ *Easy-peasy-lemon-squeezy level (page 109)*

1.  a) Lucy and Izzie
2.  b) Theresa Joanne
3.  c) Weight Winners
4.  d) Outerspaceagongalese
5.  c) Nancy No Tits
6.  a) Teen Paradise
7.  d) She is a counsellor
8.  b) Häagen-Dazs Pecan
9.  b) She is a newsreader
10. d) Rose and jasmine
11. c) Tony Costello
12. a) Scott Harris
13. d) Star Axford
14. b) Mojo
15. c) Ben and Jerry
16. a) Fat Labradors
17. c) Ben & Jerry's Chunky Monkey
18. d) King Noz
19. a) Ben
20. b) He is a lecturer in English Literature
21. b) Zac Axford, the rock star
22. a) Ollie Axford
23. c) Cyberdog
24. c) Bellini
25. d) Mark
26. b) Simon Peddington-Lee
27. d) Heddie
28. a) The Pedigree Chums
29. a) Izzie
30. c) A big lilac flower

## ★ *One-of-the-gang level (page 119)*

1.  b) Ben (lead vocalist, guitar and keyboards), Mark (bass), Elliot (keyboards), Biff (drums)
2.  b) Ben's garage, done out like an Arabian tent
3.  d) They are both doctors
4.  c) £45,000
5.  a) Candice Carter
6.  d) Elliot
7.  c) Wood Green High
8.  b) Scott Harris
9.  a) Two seconds
10. c) Ten seconds
11. d) Half Jamaican, half Italian, with a bit of Spanish thrown in – olé olé olé olé
12. d) A Pringle
13. a) *Cocktails for City Nights*
14. b) Josh Harper
15. a) Little pearl studs
16. d) Cat Kennedy
17. c) Lia
18. c) Barton Hall

19. a) Rose Harbour Cottage
20. b) *Teen Talk*
21. a) An American singer-song-writer
22. d) Gabriel
23. b) *The Snow Queen*
24. c) The Ugly Sisters

25. b) Claudia and Amelia
26. d) They are both accountants
27. a) Marisa
28. c) Sam Denham
29. d) The Aura School
30. b) A delicate bracelet of leaves on her ankle

## ★ *Friends-forever level (page 129)*

1. b) She wanted to go up to a bookshop in Muswell Hill to hear one of her favourite authors, Leila Ferrin, giving a talk
2. d) Del
3. a) Emma Ford
4. c) *Freemont News*
5. a) Mrs Dawson
6. a) Eight pounds
7. d) Mr Johnson and Mrs Elwes
8. b) Teddy Ambrosini Junior
9. c) Arianna and Cecilia
10. a) Hotel Villa Corelli
11. d) Mrs Finkelstein
12. c) Spaghetti Bolognese
13. b) Burgh Island Hotel
14. b) Sian Collins and Olivia Jacobs
15. a) Daniel
16. d) Little Bear
17. c) Montbury Lodge
18. c) Rex
19. b) She has dentures instead of her two front teeth

20. a) *Alien Mutants in Cyberspace*
21. d) So she could give all the boys the kiss of life
22. b) St Michael's
23. c) Jeremy
24. d) A calculator – the stepsister and her new husband were both accountants!
25. b) Reincarnation's making a comeback
26. b) Leister
27. a) £260 (£60 to register and £200 for a portfolio)
28. c) Mr Mackety
29. d) Eight
30. Score one point for each of these you remembered correctly: Goody Two Shoes, Awesome-Arm Annie the Female Wrestler, Noola the Alien Girl, Lola, Alice, Beryl the Bag Lady, Cassandra the Prophetess of Doom, Minnie the Mouse

## ★ *Lucy's T-shirt slogans (page 143)*

Princess, having had enough of princes, seeks frog.

God made us sisters, chocolate made us friends.

Your village phoned. They want their idiot back.

Absence makes the heart grow fonder (of somebody else).

Warning! Next mood swing in 5 minutes.

I can see clearly now my brain has gone.

Out of my mind – back in 5 minutes.

Fashion Police Academy.

When God made boys she was only joking.

Falling in love is awfully simple. Falling out of love is simply awful.

A woman needs a man like a fish needs a bicycle.

The perfect boy? One who snogs for half an hour and then turns into a pizza.

Insanity is hereditary. You get it from your kids.

As ye smoke, so shall ye reek.

## ★ *TJ's made-up books by made-up authors (page 144)*

*Modern Giants* by Hugh Mungous

*Pain in the Neck* by Lauren Gitis

*Over the Cliff* by Hugo First

*The Cat's Revenge* by Claude Bottom

*Rusty Bedsprings* by I P Nightly

*Chicken Dishes* by Nora Drumstick

*Bubbles in the Bath* by Ivor Windybottom

*A Stitch in Time* by Justin Case

*Chest Pain Remedies* by I Coffedalot

*Poo on the Wall* by Hoo Flung Dung

*Dog Bites* by R Stornaway

*Rhythm of the Night* by Mark Time

*Bad Falls* by Eileen Dover

*Chest Complaints* by Ivor Tickliecoff

*Run to the Loo* by Willie Makeit

*Body Parts* by Anne Atomy

## ★ *Lucy's mum's angel cards (page 145)*

The darkest hour is just before dawn.

Choice, not chance, determines destiny.

The tragedy in life doesn't lie in not reaching your goal. The tragedy lies in having no goal.

Don't wait for your ship to come in. Swim out to it.

The people who get on in the world are the people who get up and look for the circumstances they want. And if they can't find them, make them. (GB Shaw)

If you want a friend, be a friend.

No one can make you feel inferior without your permission.

## ★ Parent-speak (page 146)

| | |
|---|---|
| What's this lying on the floor? | This is yours. Pick it up!. |
| I need to have a word. | I'm going to tell you off. |
| That TV programme doesn't look very interesting. | Turn it off. |
| It's getting late. | Go to bed. |
| Your room's a mess. | Tidy it RIGHT NOW. |
| Are you watching this TV programme? | I want to watch something else. |
| It's time you learned how to look after yourself as I won't be around forever. | Wash up. |
| We need to talk. | You've done something wrong. |
| You must learn to communicate. | You must learn to agree with me. |
| Go ahead. (*with raised eyebrow*) | Make my day! (Warning: This is not permission – it is a dare. Be careful!) |

## ★ Boy-speak (page 147)

| | |
|---|---|
| I need space. | For my other girlfriends. |
| Let's just see how it goes. | Back off, I'm feeling pressured. |
| Would you like a back rub? | I want to grope you. |
| Isn't it warm in here? | I want to grope you and am hoping you'll take your clothes off. |
| Hi. Your friend looks nice. | I fancy her and I'm using you to get to her. |
| Don't get heavy. | I don't feel the same way about you. |
| She's ugly/a lesbian. | She didn't fancy me. |
| I'm not ready for a relationship. | At least, not with you. |
| I'm very independent. | I like my own way. |
| I think we should be free to date other people. | I already am. |
| We can still be friends. | You're history, baby. |

★ *Anagrams – The girls (page 148)*

1.  Lucy Lovering
2.  Nesta Williams
3.  Theresa Joanne Watts
4.  Izzie Foster
5.  Candice Carter
6.  Star Axford
7.  Cat Kennedy
8.  Lia Axford
9.  Tanya Peddington Lee
10. Cressida Dudley-Smythe

★ *Anagrams – The boys (page 148)*

1.  Tony Costello
2.  Lal Lovering
3.  Steve Lovering
4.  Luke De Biasi
5.  Ollie Axford
6.  Simon Peddington-Lee
7.  Josh Harper
8.  William Lewis
9.  Teddy Ambrosini-Junior
10. Scott Harris

★ *Order, order! (page 150)*

1) Mates, Dates and Inflatable Bras
2) Mates, Dates and Cosmic Kisses
3) Mates, Dates and Portobello Princesses
4) Mates, Dates and Sleepover Secrets
5) Mates, Dates and Sole Survivors
6) Mates, Dates and Mad Mistakes
7) Mates, Dates and Pulling Power
8) Mates, Dates and Tempting Trouble
9) Mates, Dates and Great Escapes
10) Mates, Dates and Chocolate Cheats
11) Mates, Dates and Diamond Destiny
12) Mates, Dates and Sizzling Summers

★ *Names and star signs (page 151)*

1. TJ Watts
2. Nesta Williams
3. Izzie Foster
4. Lucy Lovering
5. Izzie: Aquarius
6. Lucy: Gemini
7. Nesta: Leo
8. TJ: Sagittarius

★ *True or false? The parents (page 152)*

1. False – Nesta's dad drives a BMW
2. False – TJ's best mate Hannah nicknamed TJ's dad 'Scary Dad'
3. True – Izzie's stepmum is called Anna
4. False – Lucy's dad teaches the guitar
5. True – Nesta's mum's usual perfume is Ô de Lancôme

★ *True or false? London (page 153)*

1. False – Raj's is in Highgate
2. True – Izzie in particular loves Camden Lock
   because there are lots of New Age stalls and Lucy loves
   Portobello Road especially because it has so many vintage
   clothing stalls
3. False – it was called the Everyman cinema
4. False – Ruby in the Dust in Muswell Hill is Nesta's favourite
   café, not curry house!
5. True (Simon Peddington-Lee impressed Nesta with this bit of
   information on their first date)

## ★ *True or false? The boys (page 154)*

1. False – Ollie Axford's eyes were cornflower-blue
2. False – Gabriel's boyfriend was called Andy
3. True – Daniel wanted to go to the London School of Fashion to train to be a fashion designer and then go on to work in Milan or Paris
4. False – Sam Denham rode a pushbike
5. True – William Lewis had ginger hair

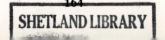

# Cathy Hopkins

## Like this book?
## Become a mate today!

# Also available by Cathy Hopkins

### The MATES, DATES series

1. Mates, Dates and Inflatable Bras
2. Mates, Dates and Cosmic Kisses
3. Mates, Dates and Portobello Princesses
4. Mates, Dates and Sleepover Secrets
5. Mates, Dates and Sole Survivors
6. Mates, Dates and Mad Mistakes
7. Mates, Dates and Pulling Power
8. Mates, Dates and Tempting Trouble
9. Mates, Dates and Great Escapes
10. Mates, Dates and Chocolate Cheats
11. Mates, Dates and Diamond Destiny
12. Mates, Dates and Sizzling Summers

*Companion Book:*
Mates, Dates Guide to Life

### The TRUTH, DARE, KISS OR PROMISE series

1. White Lies and Barefaced Truths
2. Pop Princess
3. Teen Queens and Has-Beens
4. Starstruck
5. Double Dare
6. Midsummer Meltdown
7. Love Lottery
8. All Mates Together

### The CINNAMON GIRL series

1. This Way to Paradise
2. Starting Over

**Find out more at www.piccadillypress.co.uk**
**Join Cathy's Club at www.cathyhopkins.com**